A Western Horseman Book

ROOFS
AND
RAILS

How To Plan and Build Your Ideal Horse Facility

By Gavin Ehringer

Edited by Gary Vorhes

ROOFS
AND
RAILS

Published by
Western Horseman Inc.

3850 North Nevada Ave.
Box 7980
Colorado Springs, CO 80933-7980

Design, Typography, and Production
Western Horseman
Colorado Springs, Colorado

Cover Photograph: 320 Ranch, Gallatin Gateway, Montana
Dwayne Brech

Printing
Publisher's Press
Salt Lake City, Utah

Second Printing: August 1998

ISBN 0-911647-31-7

DEDICATION

This book is dedicated to my family,
who always believed that I would become a writer, and to *WH*
Publishers Randy Witte and the late Dick Spencer, who helped
me reach my dream.

Gavin Ehringer

GAVIN EHRINGER

ACKNOWLEDGEMENTS

I would especially like to thank
Frank Klipfel of BarnTec of Colorado Springs,
for his technical assistance and advice.
Also, Billy Jack Barrett, U.S. Air Force Academy Stables;
the folks at Morton Buildings; Academy Fence Co.;
and the manufacturers of Port-A-Stall Barns.

INTRODUCTION

GOOD HORSEMANSHIP requires attention to many considerations involving the care, health, safety, and training of horses. A horseman takes as much pride in his facilities as he takes in his horses.

When planning facilities, a horseman should realize that horses' needs are fairly simple; the details are what complicate matters. In a nutshell, horses require good nutrition, daily exercise, fresh air and water, some exposure to sunlight, shelter from weather, and a clean, comfortable place to rest. Safety for both horses and people is also a vital factor.

Caring for horses' needs in a comfortable, efficient, and convenient manner should be the primary goal in designing facilities. For all but the wealthy, cost is a consideration. But even horsemen on limited budgets can provide for their horses' needs by sticking to necessities first and planning improvements in stages.

A common mistake is to build a barn or some corrals without giving thought to future improvements. As a property owner adds practice arenas, exercise pens, hot walkers, and other facilities, he may find his land overwhelmed by his growing horse operation. On a large spread, lack of planning can contribute to inefficiency and lead to costly renovation. That's why it's best to start with an overall facilities plan. By facilities, I refer to barns, storage buildings, corrals, pens, arenas, and pasture land—the infrastructure of a horse outfit. Whether you own or plan to buy raw land, or own acreage with a home but no horse facilities, working out the details before you build will save time and money in the long run. It's a lot cheaper and easier to move a building to make room for an arena when that building is on graph paper.

Because horsemen have highly varied goals and objectives, no single facility's design can meet the needs of every horseman and his livestock. Therefore, a plan that addresses your unique situation must be the starting point of an overall property management plan. This book is designed to help you in the planning process.

There are a number of factors that can affect your choices and options. Many of these subjects are covered in depth in this book. If you will be working with builders, some of these factors will be known to them. And some of these factors will require you to do some research.

Before making a detailed plan, you'll need to look into building codes, permits, zoning requirements, set-back ordinances, and all other local restrictions that apply to horses, buildings, or the use of facilities. These may include covenants, noise and animal ordinances, waste disposal requirements, ground water protection, and others. If you will be working with a builder, he should know much of this information. Another source of guidance is your regional building authority.

Besides considering the examples offered in this book, I recommend that you study barns and stables in your area. Consider the advantages and disadvantages of different materials and designs. See how some of their features would work for you. Ask neighbors what they would do differently if they were to rebuild their stables.

Plan your facilities for the number of horses you have, and consider how you could expand your facilities to add more horses in the future.

Check into your water, septic, and electrical services, and how they can be expanded to accommodate your new facilities. For safety's sake, most stables have a separate electrical circuit. You'll need a water supply—8 to 10 gallons a day per horse—plus water for grooming,

INTRODUCTION

cleaning, and fire prevention.

One horse will produce several (one source estimates 8) tons of manure a year, not counting bedding. Disposal and storage will have to conform to local regulations, or may utilize a municipal sewage system. If you own a small acreage, you may need to arrange weekly removal of manure and bedding. If you have enough land, you may be able to spread the manure as fertilizer.

If you have nearby neighbors, keep them in mind. Consider prevailing winds, offensive odors, fences, waste disposal, and insect control. Determine the total space requirements of your facilities. These may include stables, corrals, arenas, pasture areas, vehicle lanes and turnarounds, trailer parking, shop areas, and facilities for bulk feed and bedding storage.

If you are considering a horse barn, determine the proper size. A floorplan should include stalls, alleys, tack room, feed room, and storage areas. Also, you might include room for an indoor arena, office, and wash rack.

Find out about fire protection in your area. Response time, water hydrant location, water pressure and volume, and the capabilities of your fire department should be assessed. You might need to modify your plans to maximize fire safety for your facilities. For example, if you live in an area with substandard fire protection, it may be wise to build a steel barn rather than a wood barn, or to install a sprinkler fire protection system.

Weather will greatly affect design needs. Consider local weather patterns, particularly prevailing winds, precipitation patterns, annual snowfall, maximum and minimum temperatures, frost depth, and maximum wind velocities. These will influence structural design, building location, building materials, and construction.

Study your budget to determine how much you can accomplish and how much time it will take. Organizing your plans into immediate necessities, future improvements, and long-term desires can help you keep your overall project under financial control. Decide the management style best applicable to your goals and means, and the welfare of your horses. If you are a recreational trail rider, for example, your needs will be much simpler than those of a show exhibitor or a professional trainer.

Consider your objectives and resources. If you use your horses only for trail riding, you might not need a barn. You could keep them on pasture or in corrals that have a sturdy, three-sided shelter for protection against inclement weather. Or you could build a modest barn rather than an elaborate show barn.

If you are training horses for the show ring and must keep them in top condition year-round, a barn will make the work a lot easier. If horse shows are still somewhere in your future, you could build a barn to allow you to expand toward this goal.

There are certain advantages to pasturing horses. The biggest advantage is that your costs and maintenance (cleaning stalls, for example) are minimized. Pasturing horses can be more economical than stabling, and it greatly simplifies the tasks of feeding, watering, and manure management. Well-maintained and managed pastures can provide excellent nutrition for horses, although supplemental feed might be required during snowy months and in areas that produce poor quality grass.

Pastured horses are also less likely to develop respiratory problems common to some stabled horses. Because horses tend to run and play in large open areas, their needs for fresh air and some exercise are

INTRODUCTION

met. Pastured horses seldom develop vices such as wood chewing, cribbing, weaving, or pawing that sometimes occur among stabled horses.

There are some disadvantages to keeping horses on pasture. The high cost of land, particularly in urban and suburban areas, may rule out pasture. Although some people pasture a couple of horses on suburban lots of a few acres, this type of arrangement must be monitored. Horses left to themselves will eat far more than they actually need, and a small pasture will be quickly grazed to nothing. Soon the pasture will be overgrown with weeds.

Erosion may also occur during heavy rains, and the land can turn into a muddy bog.

For such small acreages, proper management means confining horses, feeding them regularly, and allowing them short periods of grazing and exercise in the pasture area.

On 2 to 5 acres, there's usually enough room for a riding arena, corrals or pens, a barn, and some pasture. However, in most areas of the country, this is just not enough room for a real pasture situation. Again, confinement and feed are necessary, as is careful attention to the condition of the land.

Acreages of 10 to 20 acres or more begin to open up possibilities for a true pasture arrangement. Cross-fencing allows the rotation of pastures and a management system that can provide year-round grazing in mild climates. However, these mid-size acreages also invite owners to buy more horses. In a variation of Murphy's Law, the more land one has, the more horses one will buy, whether one truly needs more horses or not.

In one example, a couple bought a 27-acre property in a mountainous area of the Pacific Northwest and turned a dozen Belgian draft horses loose. After only a few months, the entire pasture was overgrazed. Weeds, anthills, and eroded soil covered the once-productive pasture land. The moral: A large pasture can be overgrazed, just like a small one.

Horses kept on pasture can be difficult to catch. You must either encourage them to come to you, such as by rattling a can of oats, or you must go get them. In bad weather, it can be inconvenient to saddle your horse and ride. This can result in disenchantment for the horse owner and less regular exercise for the horse.

In cold climates, a horse kept outdoors will grow a thick winter coat. A short ride can cause the horse to sweat, and without proper cool-down and grooming, the horse can experience health problems.

Most horsemen with small acreages find that stables, runs, and corrals are a necessity. So do performance and show horse operations, as well as breeding establishments. The principal advantage of stables is that they provide a controlled environment that facilitates grooming and care while providing shelter from weather extremes.

However, the stabled horse relies totally on his owner for feed, water, a clean stall, and exercise. Keeping a horse in a stable is labor-intensive, and will require far more of the horseman's time than a pasture arrangement.

A well-built stable is a product of the builder's attention to details. These include: proper ventilation, natural and electric lighting, building materials, space requirements, water, feed storage, tack storage, fire safety, and safety of the horses and the people involved. Each of these issues will be discussed in the following chapters.

—*Gavin Ehringer*

CONTENTS

BUILDING TYPE AND SITE

1

Your needs and budget should guide your planning.

WHETHER YOU build a barn yourself or hire a professional builder for the project, knowing your options will help you to personalize your stable and create a building ideally suited to your needs and tastes.

In this chapter, we will look at barn building from the ground up, considering various building types. The idea is to help you visualize the kind of building you want. We'll also help you pick the best site for that building.

Type

The type of stable you build will depend entirely on your personal needs and on your budget. A stable can be as simple and inexpensive as a 12 by 12-foot shed built of scrap lumber and plywood, or it can be as elegant as your checkbook and imagination will allow.

However, there are four basic stable designs.

A center-aisle barn with runs on each stall. Note that the roof extends over part of each run.

10

1/ The center-aisle stable, with a row of stalls on either side of an aisle. This is a very popular style. It offers a place for grooming and other chores during bad weather, whether that means rain and snow or sizzling heat.

A center-aisle barn can be as small as three stalls, with, for example, two on one side plus another stall and a tack-feed room on the other. Or it can be as large as 20 or more stalls on each side.

Some of the biggest buildings have the tack rooms and grooming areas in the middle part of the barn. Some have packed dirt aisles wide enough to allow riders to exercise horses indoors during bad weather. One elaborate California stable even incorporated a round pen at each end of the extremely long center aisle.

2/ The shed-row barn, in which all stalls face one direction. Often the roof extends over a walkway in front of the stalls to provide weather protection and a place for grooming, doctoring, or saddling. A feed room and tack room can be incorporated into the design. The shed-row design can be modified into an L-shape to make stall servicing more centralized and efficient. Shed-row barns are popular among people with just two or three horses or who don't want an elaborate facility.

This inexpensive structure houses two horses with a divider between. They share an automatic waterer.

There are a number of innovative barns and shelters that don't fall into one of the four basic styles.

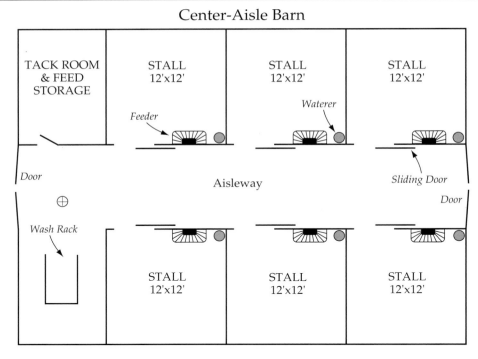

Center-Aisle Barn

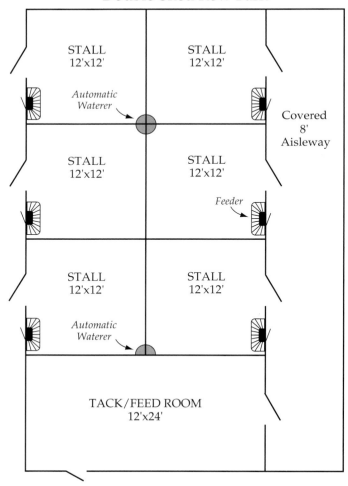

Double-Shed Row Barn

3/ The double-sided shed-row barn, with stalls placed back-to-back, and often with an aisle around the perimeter. This type is common at racetracks in milder climates and at fairgrounds and other horse show facilities. Double-sided shed-row barns usually require less materials to construct than center-aisle barns, which is one reason for their popularity at tracks and show grounds.

4/ The loafing shed, so named because it offers a place for pastured or corralled horses to loaf out of the rain, snow, wind, and sun. It is very economical to build, as it has only three sides and a roof.

If pastured horses are fed supplemental hay and grain, a grain trough and hayrack can be built along the walls of the loafing shed. Some shed owners build a storage room along the back to store hay and grain, thus making feeding chores easier.

There are a number of innovative barns and shelters that don't fall into the four basic styles. These include round barns, with stalls on the perimeter with an aisle in front of them and a walking ring or longeing area in the center. A round barn, however, is one of the most expensive types to build.

Some horsemen add shelters to the side of an existing building, such as a garage. The material savings can be considerable.

3-Stall Shed with adjoining runs

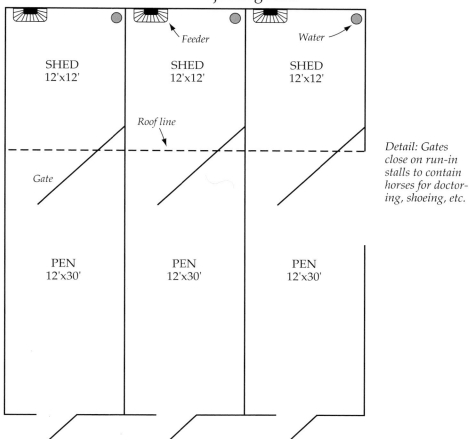

Feeder

Water

SHED
12'x12'

SHED
12'x12'

SHED
12'x12'

Roof line

Gate

PEN
12'x30'

PEN
12'x30'

PEN
12'x30'

*Detail: Gates
close on run-in
stalls to contain
horses for doctor-
ing, shoeing, etc.*

**The most important
consideration is
simply to provide
some sort of shelter
for your horse or
horses.**

However, manure management and fly control can be irritating if the lean-to shed or stable is too close to the home. The most important consideration is simply to provide some sort of shelter for your horse or horses. In warm climates, such as Florida, the most important consideration is shelter from heavy rains and a scorching hot sun. In Montana, a windbreak is the most important aspect. Most horses don't object to falling snow, but when a cold wind begins knifing through, they will seek a windbreak wherever they can find one—in thick brush, a creek bottom, or even a solitary power-line pole.

Site

Selecting a site will greatly affect the comfort and efficiency of your operation, as well as the cost of construction.

The main factors to consider in selecting a site are weather, drainage, soil conditions,

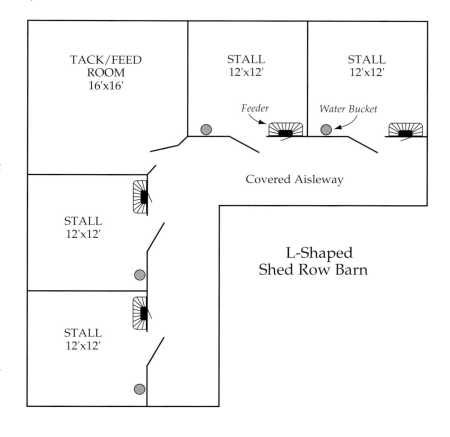

TACK/FEED
ROOM
16'x16'

STALL
12'x12'

STALL
12'x12'

Feeder

Water Bucket

Covered Aisleway

STALL
12'x12'

L-Shaped
Shed Row Barn

STALL
12'x12'

A back-to-back shed-row building, with all stalls opening to the outside.

This loafing shed on an Oklahoma horse farm serves two broodmare pastures.

Round barns are fairly rare. Note the cupola for ventilation.

Weather patterns in your area must be taken into account in selecting your building site.

ease of service, and local building requirements. Zoning regulations and building codes can vary greatly. Since these requirements may restrict your options, you need to check on them first. Before you begin planning your stable and looking for a site, pick up the phone and call the local regional building department regarding zoning and building codes. Also, check property deeds, easements, setback requirements, and covenants for restrictions that may apply to your property.

Weather patterns in your area must be taken into account in selecting your building site. Determine what weather conditions you'll need to protect your horses from, and how best to accommodate extremes of weather. If you recently purchased your property, it's worthwhile to pay attention to weather conditions over the course of a year.

One couple bought a property in the fall, built their barn in the winter, and in June discovered that they'd located it atop a natural spring. Even costly excavation failed to divert the stream that ran right through the center of their barn. A little patience and observation could have saved them a great deal of inconvenience.

In hot, southern locales, protecting your stable from heat and direct sunlight may dictate that you place your building on the north slope of a hill, or under shade trees. In snowy northern climates, placing the building on a south-facing, treeless slope can help minimize snow accumulation and provide more sunshine to warm the building and the horses.

It's usually best to face the main building or buildings away from severe prevailing winds. An exception may be made in areas with heavy seasonal storms that follow their own patterns.

In areas where winds tend to come from the north, northwest, or west, buildings should generally face south or southeast.

In regions where winds mainly blow out of the south, buildings should generally be oriented north. However, local topography may affect the climate in your area. If you're uncertain of local weather patterns, check with a meteorologist or other local weather authority for specific information.

Even in cold climates, a horse gets along fine with basic protection from wind, such as that provided by this run-in stall.

Topography and soil conditions determine the quality of drainage.

If you are new to an area, don't rely on neighbors (especially if they don't own horses) to tell you from which direction the storms come. In one instance, a newcomer to Colorado built a loafing shed facing north after being told by neighbors (not horse owners) that the prevailing breezes came from the south. Well, that was true, but most of the winter storms came from the north.

Good drainage will help prevent local flooding and damage to driveways and building foundations. It also provides adequate leaching for underground septic systems. Topography and soil conditions determine the quality of drainage.

If possible, choose a relatively level building site to save on costly excavation. Ideally, the ground should slope downward slightly on all sides of the building at a 2 to 6 percent grade. That is, the ground should lose 2 to 6 feet of elevation per 100 feet of linear area. A steeper grade can result in erosion problems.

If the area is not naturally well-drained, it is advisable to place the barn on an earthen pad 6 to 12 inches higher than the surrounding land. The pad helps divert water away from the building foundation. This is generally accomplished by expanding the pad 10 feet wider than the barn "footprint" (the area actually covered) and backfilling the area with a bed of 1-inch rock, 6 to 8 inches deep. The rocks are then covered with a heavy material such as dirt. In many cases, the pad can be built up from dirt available on site. This is the least costly solution.

If flooding is a possibility, you may need to develop an even higher pad, although even the minimal height is adequate for most circumstances. In areas where surface drainage is inadequate and

This two-story structure houses hay, grain, and trailer above with two box stalls below that open into pens.

Site selection should always consider drainage. Before having this barn built, the owner was unaware that the site was subject to flooding from runoff water during heavy rains and from melting snow. That's not a regular stream in the background; it's just runoff water. Fortunately, the flooding doesn't happen very often, and it has never gotten into the barn.

standing water remains for days after a rainstorm, it may be necessary to improve the percolation of surface water using subterranean drains.

Flooding might not seem like a possibility if the location is not close to a stream bed. But flooding can occur from runoff water in heavy rain storms or from melting snow. So before building, check the drainage pattern in the area you plan to build the barn.

In hilly terrain, building on a slope may be necessary. If so, water can be diverted away from the building with a raised site pad, a drainage ditch on the uphill side, or a berm created during excavation.

Soil conditions greatly affect the permeability of the ground, as well as the stability of the construction site. For all practical purposes, sandy soils are best. Sand not only provides better drainage than loamy soil or clay, it is also the most stable building substratum.

Clay, often preferred by horsemen for stall floors, can cause problems in construction. Clay is referred to in the trade as a "hot" material, because it is expansive.

In a pole barn, expanding clay can exert as much as five times the force on a buildings' support poles as the building weight itself. In fact, clay is so expansive that it can literally push a building around.

In the case of clay soils, the least expensive method of pole barn construction is to drill holes below the level of the clay and anchor the support poles in a more stable substratum. Another method is to excavate the clay and backfill the area with a more stable soil. Some sites require a construction method called *slab on grade*, in which a poured concrete slab—and sometimes the building itself—actually floats atop the unstable ground.

A soil evaluation will determine the types of soils underlying your prospective site. If there are expansive soils in the area, you'll learn that from a soil test. A construction engineer can help determine the best method of construction for your soil conditions.

Situating your barn next to your home may seem sensible, considering the daily chores of feeding, watering, cleaning stalls, and exercising your horses. But a barn too close to the house also results in lots of flies, not to mention the smell of what attracted them in the first place.

For the sake of sanitation and fire safety,

Here's a nice three-stall facility that's good for horses who cannot be ridden or exercised every day. Each stall opens into a large pen.

a barn should be at least 100 feet from your living quarters. If manure is to be temporarily stored on the premises, a containment area isolated from natural drainage areas should be planned. It should be downwind from both your home and any neighboring houses. There may be local regulations regarding the storage and disposal of animal wastes.

In assessing the quality of a site, also consider the space required for runs, pens, hay storage, trailer storage, and overall accessibility. Will there be sufficient turn-around room for a truck and trailer? Is the place where you plan to store hay and bedding accessible to delivery vehicles? Will there be room for expansion? Will paddocks, pastures, corrals, and arenas be easily accessible to the barn area? Water and electricity must be provided at the barn site, whether from public systems or private ones. It is advisable to put barns and outbuildings on a separate electrical circuit. All these factors need to be addressed in a comprehensive plan for your facilities, present and future.

CONSTRUCTION STYLES

Choose one of three basic kinds of buildings.

MOST HORSE barns are of pole, stud frame, masonry, or metal construction. Pole barns are built on poles or posts buried in the ground; stud frame barns utilize wood frames made of dressed or rough lumber; masonry barns are made of brick, stone, poured concrete, or mortared concrete blocks. Of these three types, the pole barn is the least costly and one of the most popular.

Pole Barns

The main savings in a pole barn are in the foundation work. Pole barns are built on a foundation of poles or posts set 4 to 8 feet in the ground. Generally, the poles are anchored by concrete collars, or they may simply rest on a small concrete pad. Once the site preparation is complete, excavation only involves the careful placing of the holes in which the poles will be

set. A tractor equipped with a power auger is often used for this work. In the case of small barns or hard-to-reach sites, this work can even be performed by hand, using a post-hole digger.

This simple foundation system offers significant cost savings over the concrete pads used in conventional stud frame or masonry buildings. Wall foundations require extensive excavation, as well as skilled laborers to build forms and pour the concrete for footings and foundation walls. For example, a 36 by 42-foot barn with a foundation 4 feet deep would require about 22 cubic yards of concrete; the same size pole barn would use less than a single yard.

The added expenses of a wall foundation can add 10 to 15 percent to a barn's cost.

Another advantage concerns the way a pole barn is framed. The weight of roofs,

A commercially built pole building with metal siding.

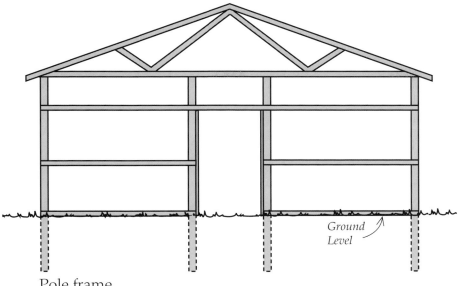

Pole frame.

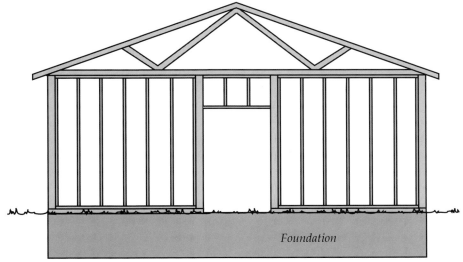

Stud wall frame.

Because the walls of a pole barn are not load-bearing, they can be constructed of light materials.

lofts, and exterior walls is supported by the poles. Because the walls are not load-bearing, they can be constructed of light materials. This offers a great deal of flexibility in wall placement. With relative ease, the owner can remove, reposition, or add walls and modify floor plans to accommodate changes in management needs. Furthermore, large doors and windows can be used in pole buildings because their frames do not have to support heavy structural loads, as is the case in stud frame and masonry buildings.

Despite the simple frames, properly engineered pole buildings can be quite strong. Since the frame and foundation are an integral unit that is embedded in the earth, the energy from forces such as tornado winds and flood waters is trans-

ferred through the poles into the ground, where it dissipates.

Because poles are the structural framework of a pole barn, they must be protected from wood-chewing horses. This is generally done by covering the poles with boards, or by wrapping exposed poles with wire mesh or thin sheet metal.

These photographs show the progression of a pole building. It can be covered with any type of siding. A foundation is not necessary.

Brick is used in combination with some wood under a metal and fiberglass roof on this Arizona barn. The fiberglass saves on electricity while keeping the aisleway well lighted.

Stud Frame Barns

Builders commonly use stud frame construction for homes. The primary advantage of a stud frame barn is that residential contractors often have more experience with this type of building. In areas where there are no pole building specialists, you may be limited to this type of barn.

In stud frame construction, 2 by 4- or 2 by 6-inch studs are joined in a framework that is erected on a floor platform. Each board supports a small portion of the building's roof and upper levels, and is therefore structurally important. For the do-it-yourself barn builder working by himself, stud frames can be easier to erect.

A single person can frame the building because it has light components. In contrast, a large pole barn may require two or three men to wrestle heavy poles into position.

It is possible to build a stud-frame barn on a pole foundation. Some contractors who do not specialize in pole construction may be willing to build a platform-style barn on a pole foundation to save on excavation costs.

To take this a step further, some pole barn builders may use stud framing between the poles. In this way, they can utilize standard building materials designed for stud-frame buildings as well as to enclose insulation, electrical wiring, and plumbing in the walls. The frame also adds extra rigidity to the walls, a blessing during a heavy storm that might shake the walls of a conventional pole barn. The studs may be attached to the horizontal girts, which are horizontal boards that span the poles and provide nailing surfaces. The technique is called girt bracing. Otherwise, the stud frame may be attached directly to the poles or posts.

Masonry Barns

The appeal of masonry barns is more aesthetic than practical. Buildings of brick, concrete block, adobe, or stone are expensive, both in materials and labor. Poured concrete buildings can be relatively cheap, but generally are less attractive than barns of other material. Masonry buildings are less of a fire danger, which can save on insurance. But insurance savings hardly balance out the huge cost differential between masonry barns and wood-frame barns. As one insurance agent noted, the quality and location of fire departments influences insurance rates far more than the materials used in construction.

However, many horse farms spare no expense in constructing fireproof masonry barns to protect their valued breeding and show stock. In these cases, the potential

Metal Buildings

Steel buildings are pre-engineered by a number of national manufacturers. In most cases they are erected on a foundation of steel girders set on poured concrete piers. Trusses, either wood or steel, are bolted onto the girders and support the roof. In most cases, the building shell is finished with sheet metal siding, which may be finished with a factory-painted coating.

The main advantage of a steel building is its durability. A properly engineered steel building can last 50 or more years with minimum upkeep. For buildings such as arenas that require clear spans of more than 50 feet, steel buildings are less expensive to build than any other type of building. For buildings with clear spans of less than 50 feet, steel buildings are roughly equal in price to pole or stud frame buildings. Like masonry structures, all-steel buildings are virtually fireproof.

On the down side, steel buildings require more insulation than their most popular rival, wood. An uninsulated steel barn can be noisy in a rainstorm or high wind, not to mention cold in the winter and hot in summer. Low-cost steel buildings are usually very plain and utilitarian in appearance, and do not lend themselves to modification. Some manufacturers offer a range of functional and cosmetic options that mimic features common to wood barns, but these can add substantially to the cost.

If you are considering a steel building, be certain to look into the quality control of the manufacturer. Try to find owners of similar barns in your area and get their opinions about the overall quality of their barns. Quality control can vary greatly from manufacturer to manufacturer and even from building crew to crew. It's well worth your while to compare companies before deciding on a particular steel barn. Steel buildings require precision construction, and most factory dealers recommend professional builders. Some require them.

This training barn at the Lazy E Ranch at Guthrie, Okla., is virtually fireproof because of its poured concrete walls and steel mesh partitioning between stalls. That's Orren Mixer, the renowned equine portrait artist from Edmond, Okla., indicating the texture in the finish of the concrete.
Photo by Pat Close

loss of expensive horses justifies the cost of building a fireproof masonry barn. But for the average horse owner, the expense may be hard to justify. It is prudent, however, to consider fire-retardant materials in the construction of any barn.

Masonry barns can be cool in warm climates, but cold and damp in cold climates. Mechanical ventilation is generally necessary to make masonry buildings suitable for horses.

An all-metal building is the ultimate in fire safety.

Wood is used in this barn under a metal framework.

These barns combine masonry, metal, and wood.

A clear-span arena under construction.

Timber-Frame

Timber-frame construction is one of the most universal and ancient forms of building. Once popular throughout America, timber-frame buildings passed from fashion in the late 19th century because of the mass production of nails, which simplified joinery, and because of the availability of milled lumber, which standardized building practices.

Many excellent examples of century-old timber-frame barns can still be seen in America today, a testimony to the strength and durability of timber-frame building. Partly because of its rustic appeal, and partly because of its durability and economy, timber-frame building is enjoying a modest revival.

In many cases, timber-frame builders use green lumber that is neither finished nor cured. Green lumber sells for as little as a third of the cost of kiln-dried lumber.

Like pole buildings, timber-frame structures rely on heavy poles or posts as structural supports, allowing for clear spans and non-load-bearing walls. This makes them attractive for barns, which usually require large openings and open floor space.

Timber-frame building, also called post-and-beam construction, involves the use of vertical frame units, called bents, tied together with horizontal beams known as plates. The bents and beams are stiffened and made rigid with the addition of angled braces.

Traditionally, carpenters assembled the frame members with carefully cut mortise-and-tenon joints. The mortise is a cavity or slot cut into a piece of wood; the tenon is the reduced end of another piece of wood that fits into the mortise. Fasteners, such as nails and bolts, are not used in traditional timber-frame construction. Instead, wooden pegs and wedges hold the jointed pieces together. The technique is still practiced by devotees of the craft, most notably members of the Amish religion.

Modern timber-frame buildings may have mortise-and-tenon joinery, or they may rely on metal brackets and bolts to hold the pieces together. It is worthwhile to seek out a builder with extensive experience in timber-frame construction if you wish to build this type barn, or if you plan to restore an existing timber-frame building.

Because each timber-frame building is essentially handmade, there is a great deal of personality to them.

SIDING

3

T 1-11 siding is durable, attractive, and easy to install.

SIDING AND roofing materials have the biggest impact on the appearance of your barn, and should be carefully chosen. Personal taste, durability, and cost are the main considerations in selecting siding roofing materials.

Before deciding on the overall look of your barn, it helps to study the various types of horse facilities in your area. Not only will this help in selecting exterior building materials, it will help in planning the layout and equipment of your own stable.

A neighbor with a wood-sided barn may brag on the beauty of his stable, but complain of having to paint it every few years and of replacing boards that have been damaged by his horses or by insects. Another may show you a steel barn that was once chocolate brown, but has faded to dusty tan on the southern side and has a few bent panels.

It is important to consider siding and roofing materials in terms of the shape and design of your barn and also of your home. What will look right? An all-steel barn may meet your requirements for durability, but would look awkward next to a Santa Fe-style stucco home. Likewise, a rough-plank pole barn might seem appropriately rustic next to a log home, but would look out of place in a neighborhood of modern suburban houses.

Wood siding is traditional for barns, and remains a popular choice among horsemen. Wood is also a good insulator and has an attractive appearance that complements most homes. Prices for wood siding vary greatly and are dependent on quality and availability.

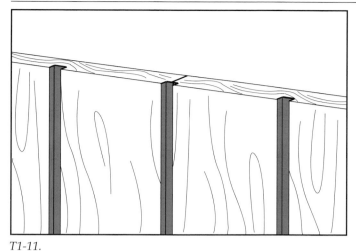
T1-11.

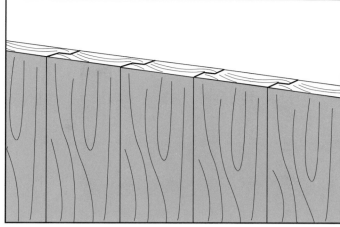
Shiplap.

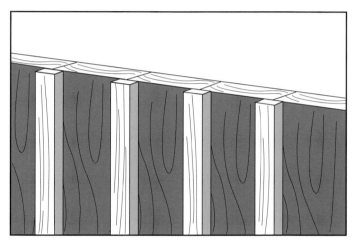
Board and batten.

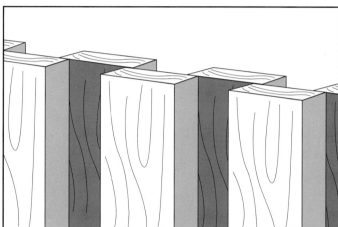
Board and board.

Generally, hardwoods weather better than softwoods and are preferred for barn exteriors. Cedar and redwood have the advantages of excellent resistance to weathering, but are relatively costly. White pine, hemlock, spruce, and Douglas fir provide good durability and are less expensive.

Pole-frame and timber-frame barns are often sided with green or native lumber. Green wood is rough-sawn lumber that comes directly from a mill or is milled on site. It usually costs from one-third to two-thirds the price of kiln-dried, dimensioned lumber. Because it is not dried or dimensioned, it can be heavy and hard to work with. Green lumber can be as much as 50 percent water by weight, and insulated walls must be allowed to breathe for 6 months before a vapor barrier can be installed. Green wood is nearly impossible to paint, and in most cases it is left natural or stained. A wood preservative is used to retain a fresh look.

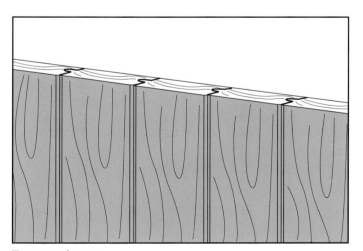
Tongue and groove.

Traditional wood siding on an older-style barn.

Another disadvantage of green lumber: As it dries, it may warp, and nails may pop out.

For siding, plywood is nearly as popular as plank boards. Its low cost and ease of use are obvious advantages, but plywood offers other benefits as well. In the first place, it adds lateral support to frame members. This is particularly important in stud-frame buildings, where plywood sheathing braces the stud frame against lateral movement. In stud-frame buildings, sheathing is usually required as a nail base for siding and serves as an air barrier. Builders generally use half-inch plywood as sheathing. However, if plywood is chosen as siding, there is no need for sheathing.

The most common exterior plywood siding is known as Texture 1-11 or T 1-11.

Dollar for dollar, it's a siding material hard to beat. This plywood product is an exterior-grade laminate whose outer layer is milled with $\frac{1}{4}$-inch grooves spaced 4 to 8 inches on center. Generally, the $\frac{5}{8}$-inch thickness is used for barns. Its texture can be smooth, brushed, or rough. A rough cedar-like finish is especially popular. Texture 1-11 can also be ordered in redwood, southern yellow pine, Douglas fir, and other woods. Textured plywood can be painted or stained like regular wood siding. It has the appearance of shiplap board siding, at a substantially lower cost.

We have discussed all-steel buildings, but we also must consider sheet-metal siding. Sheet metal can be used on most common barn frames—pole, stud, or timber-frame—as well as all-steel prefab or custom frames. Sheet-metal siding is durable, doesn't have to be painted, and is a big factor in fire safety.

However, it can be a real horse hazard. Horses who come in contact with its sharp

metal edges can be lacerated. Interior stall panels should be built to prevent horses from kicking or bending sheet metal panels, and the panels should be inspected regularly for protruding edges that could cut a horse. A horse who kicks through sheet metal will seriously cut his legs.

When sheet metal siding is used, stall walls must be covered with 2-inch-thick wood planks or ¾-inch plywood to a height of at least 4 feet from the stall floor. Any sheet metal less than 28 gauge is unacceptable for a horse barn or shed, because horses have no trouble bending or kicking holes in the lighter gauge sheets. The heavier gauge has a wind rating of 175 miles per hour, and exceeds the recommended wind-load ratings throughout the country.

Many rural buildings are sided with corrugated steel panels. Corrugated is the least expensive style of sheet metal used for barns, windbreaks, and three-sided horse sheds. Paint can't stick well to corrugated steel, and its light oil coating wears off quickly, which usually results in oxidization and rusting. Aesthetically, it is

not an attractive siding, but it is very inexpensive. Corrugated steel with a galvanized coating will outlast non-coated steel and is recommended for exterior siding.

One word of caution about corrugated steel, or any sheet metal: The bottom edges should be secured to 2 by 6s. Otherwise, the exposed sharp edge could literally cut a horse's foot off if it should slide under the edge. Exposed top edges should be similarly protected or else a horse could cut his throat on them.

Designed steel panels are the next step up from corrugated steel. They come in a number of designs. Some are made to resemble wood board siding; others have ribbed designs. They can be purchased from a manufacturer, a building supply house, or as part of a barn kit from a prefab barn company. The panels are shipped with a factory paint job, and a selection of colors is usually available. Generally, the white and off-white colors fade less and are recommended.

Commercial metal buildings come with color options.

Large arena and storage buildings are usually metal.

If you choose steel panels as siding, make sure that the materials you order are treated to prevent rust and have an ultra-violet inhibitor to prevent the paint from fading in the sun. Galvalume is the trade name of a commonly used rust prevention process. In this process, the formed sheets are first treated with a zinc-phosphate coating to improve the bonding of the primer coat and to prevent rusting. After priming, a top coat of silicone-polyester paint is applied.

No matter how good the paint process, scratches and dents can expose the base metal to weather, oxidation, and rusting. In a metal barn, as with a car, it's best to touch up scratches soon after they occur.

If you're looking for a low-maintenance siding and cost is not a concern, vinyl is the last word in siding materials. Vinyl siding is durable, easily cleaned, and never needs painting. It is available in many colors and designs, and provides extra insulation.

Quality vinyl siding includes ultra-violet inhibitors to prevent fading, although after many years, some fading can be expected. Horses don't care for the taste of plastic and usually will not crib on vinyl.

The main disadvantage of vinyl siding is its cost. It is among the most expensive siding materials, and to ensure proper weather sealing, professional installation is required. Like the wood lap siding it often resembles, vinyl siding is installed on plywood sheathing and is most suitable for stud-frame buildings. However, it can be successfully installed on pole-frame barns, provided the underlayment is skillfully done.

Some horse owners have tried stucco siding, with mixed results. Stucco is a plaster material that is applied over a plywood or masonry wall to give an adobe-like appearance. It comes in a variety of colors, and is especially pleasing when coupled with a home with a similar finish.

However, horses can easily damage stucco's fragile surface. In most situations, stucco is not up to the rugged demands of a horse barn.

A wood-frame New Mexico stable with a stucco exterior and false vegas along the roof line to create a Santa Fe look. The four stalls are of pre-engineered metal around which a wood frame structure was built. However, the horses can't get at any wood to chew.

A textured stucco exterior with metal windows and grills.

ROOFS

Climate, cost, and aesthetics influence roof choices.

MODERN HORSE barns are primarily single-story buildings with either clear-span truss designs or beam-supported rafter roofs. The popularity of single-story buildings reflects current stable management philosophies and practical cost considerations. Although the high-ceiling designs of traditional barns are attractive, these two-story structures require more materials and construction time.

Furthermore, the once-common practice of storing hay in roomy mows located above the ground-floor stable area has been largely abandoned in favor of separate hay storage facilities. Storing hay outdoors or in separate, well-ventilated buildings built for that purpose reduces fire danger to livestock and is less costly and labor-intensive than overhead storage.

The most popular roof design for modern horse facilities is the gable roof, a triangular design with two equal pitches that meet in a line at the center. This simple and relatively inexpensive design is adaptable to many floor plans and layouts. It is used for both narrow and wide stables and is suitable for closed and open buildings. By extending the roof line beyond the side walls, the builder can create outside shed areas or covered ways.

Rafters or trusses supported on wall plates or posts are used for gable-roofed buildings up to 72 feet wide. Ceilings may follow the roof line, or they may be framed to the height of the walls, with an attic storage area above. Builders often

Interlocking asphalt shingles are used on this roof.

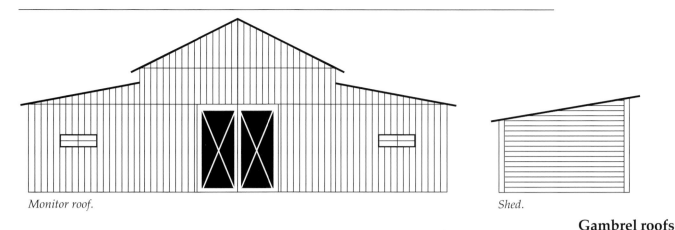

Monitor roof.

Shed.

employ clear-span trusses of steel or laminated wood to create gable roofs 100 feet or more in width. This application is most commonly used for indoor arenas.

Gable roofs may be modified to provide natural light through the use of translucent fiberglass panels or skylights built into the roof.

The offset gable is a triangular roof of two equal slopes, similar to the gable, but with one short pitch and another elongated pitch. They meet at a line located off center. Offset gables are common to single-row barn designs with a single alley, or as a gable roof with an overhanging extension. The offset gable roof may be built on posts and beams, rafters supported on walls, or on trusses.

A monitor roof is made up of a gable-roofed center section with shed roofs on both sides. The center section may be wider than the shed sections, or vice-versa. Generally, monitor roofs are not used on buildings narrower than 36 feet. Many monitor roofs feature louvers, windows, or openings in the walls below the eaves of the center section to provide natural light and ventilation. The design has a traditional appeal, as it is often associated with dairy barns seen throughout the country.

Gambrel roofs are most commonly associated with the old-time barn architecture of the Northeast and Midwest. They consist of four roof sections: two moderately pitched sections that meet at the top ridge, and two more steeply pitched sections on either side. Gambrel roofs are especially well-suited to two-story buildings. In most cases, the second story is used as a hayloft. Some people have successfully renovated old gambrel-roofed barns as homes, and others utilize the upper loft area for studios, offices, or storage areas.

Gambrel roofs are especially well-suited to two-story buildings.

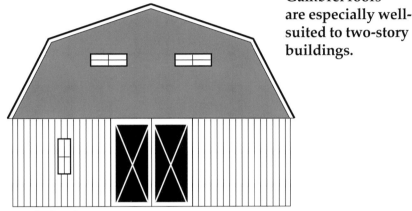

Gambrel roof.

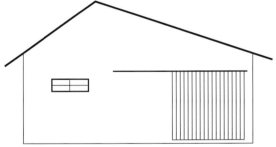

Offset gable (salt box).

Gable roof.

Shake-shingle roofs are attractive.

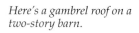

Here's a gambrel roof on a two-story barn.

*A monitor roof aids venti-
lation and lighting.*

*An offset gable roof with
sheltering overhang.*

A roof on a round pen makes it usable in almost any weather.

Steep gambrel roofs are well-suited to handle heavy snow.

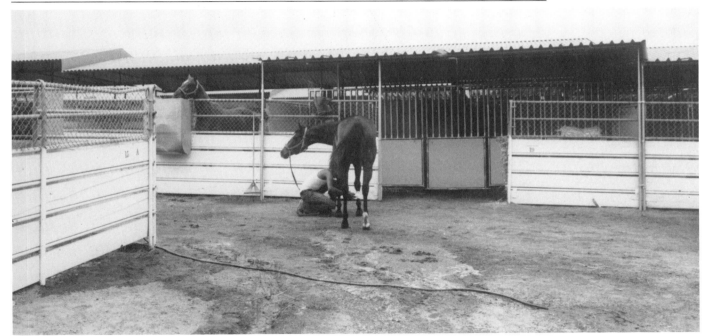

Simple corrugated metal roofs offer economy and durability.

However, the high-ceilinged gambrel roof is costly, requiring more materials and labor than the simpler shed roof, gable, or monitor designs. And the difficulty and fire danger of storing hay on the second floor makes a large gambrel-roofed barn less than desirable for a modern horse barn.

Gambrel roofs are most commonly framed with clear-span, braced rafters anchored to the mow floor joists and supported by the barn walls.

Gothic roofs are built of two arched sections that join at the ridge line. They are most often used for two-story buildings, and, like gambrel roofs, provide maximum storage space on the upper floor. The gothic roof can also be found on small, free-standing shelters.

Framing for gothic roofs generally consists of segmented rafters for smaller structures, and laminated wood rafters for buildings 40 or more feet wide.

Roofing Materials

Cedar or redwood shakes are some of the most beautiful roofing materials, and can last many years. They provide good insulation, are quiet, and prevent condensation buildup. However, they are expensive and their installation is costly—on average, wood shakes are about four times as expensive as asphalt shingles. They also present a fire hazard and can raise insurance rates. Scheduled treatments with a fire-retardant will help minimize the danger.

Asphalt shingles are common to both barns and residences. They are inexpensive and, when properly installed, can last 30 years or more. Asphalt shingles help insulate the roof from noise and heat, but are susceptible to weather damage. Common styles are overlapping shingle rows (three-tab shingles) and T-lock shingles. T-locks, although more expensive, offer an interesting patterned look and are less likely to be weather-damaged.

Another asphalt shingle product is a three-dimensional shingle that can have the

Gable roofs in warm climates need less slope than those in snowfall areas.

Traditional barns, such as this one in Missouri, often had hip sheds on each side.

appearance of wood shakes at about one-third the cost. Also available is rolled asphalt roofing material. It is acceptable for barn roofing, but is not as durable or watertight as the other asphalt roofing materials.

Metal roofs are long-lasting, easy to install, and almost maintenance-free. Depending on the quality of materials, finishes, and installation, metal roofs can last from 15 to 50 years with very little upkeep. However, uninsulated metal roofs can be hot in sunny weather and can trap moisture if not properly ventilated. Metal roofs are also noisy in rain and hail storms and may leak around fastening holes.

Corrugated sheet metal is inexpensive, but as a roofing material, it has the same drawbacks as when used for siding. Namely it is not particularly attractive, cannot be painted, and will eventually lose its coating and rust. It is also hot and noisy if it isn't insulated.

Factory-painted steel or aluminum sheets offer a more pleasing appearance than corrugated sheets and complement most varieties of siding. Heavy-gauge sheets are required for areas with high wind loads, and the specifications are generally set forth in regional building codes.

Snow collects on metal roofs, then sloughs off in a sort of mini-avalanche. Doors and entry areas need to be planned with this in mind. Steep pitches hold less snow than shallow pitches.

An efficient structure that shelters from rain and sun but utilizes natural ventilation.

Installing a skylight in a stable roof.

FLOORS AND BEDDING

IN MOST horse barns, more than one type of flooring material is used. Although a simple earthen floor can be used throughout the barn, many horse owners employ different materials in stalls, aisleways, tack rooms, and feed rooms.

Because concrete is rodent-proof and long-lasting, many horsemen choose it for tack rooms and feed storage areas. Offices, lounges, and wash rooms may have different flooring needs. Generally, wash rooms require textured concrete floors; tack rooms, lounges, and offices might have wood, concrete, or covered plywood flooring.

Stall and Aisleway Floors

The main considerations for stall flooring are durability and ease of sanitation. Hard surfaces that lack elasticity, such as concrete, are hard on horses' legs. To get around this problem, cushioning materials such as deep bedding or rubber stall mats must be used.

Dirt is probably the most common flooring material for horse stalls, and it comes closest to approximating a horse's natural footing. The main advantage, of course, is that it costs nothing if there is good dirt available at the building site. Furthermore, dirt is absorbent, provides good footing, and is easy on horses' legs.

But there are drawbacks. Dirt can stay wet for long periods, is nearly impossible to sanitize, and must be regraded frequently. In cold climates, dirt can freeze and make stall cleaning difficult.

Horsemen sometimes choose sand as a stall flooring material because of its high absorbency and because it is easy on horses' legs. However, its disadvantages

A big-capacity cart is handy for bedding and cleaning stalls.

Chart of Flooring Materials

Material	Characteristics	Ease of Sanitation	Suggested Uses	Relative Cost
Hardwood	Easy on legs, durable, attractive, low-maintenance, can be slippery	Moderate	Aisleways, tack room, office	Expensive
Pinewood	Easy on legs, attractive, slippery, wears more quickly than hardwood, may splinter	Moderate	Aisleways, tack room, office	Moderate
Clay	Easy on legs, may dry hoofs, needs frequent replacement, can be slick and oily	Difficult	Stalls	Inexpensive
Dirt	Closest to natural footing, high maintenance, easy on legs, can freeze in winter	Difficult	Aisleways, stalls	Least expensive
Plywood (¾ - 1" flooring)	Durable, low-maintenance, often used as carpet underlayment	Moderate, seldom used for stall floors	Tack and feed room	Moderate
Sand	Use may lead to sand colic, can cause hoof problems, needs daily stall maintenance	Moderate	Arenas only	Inexpensive
Concrete	Hard on legs, stalls require deep bedding or mats; must be textured, rodent-proof; durable	Easy	Stalls, aisleways, tack and feed rooms, wash areas, offices	Expensive when done professionally
Asphalt	Susceptible to weather damage, needs replacement in 3 - 5 years, softer than concrete	Easy	Stalls, aisleways, tack and feed rooms, service roads	Expensive in small applications
Road base or coarse aggregate rock	Easy to level, requires maintenance unless topped with rubber mats, easy to install	Moderate	Stalls, aisleways, service roads, wash areas	Inexpensive
Rubber stall mats or rubber bricks	Maintenance free, durable; easy on legs, should be used with road base or concrete floors, saves bedding	Easy	Stalls, aisleways, wash areas	Expensive

must be considered. Sand can dry a horse's hoofs. In some cases, sand can work into the hoof wall and cause serious and sometimes permanent damage. If the horse eats feed off the floor, ingesting sand can lead to colic. For these reasons, sand is a poor choice for stall flooring.

Clay is a popular stall flooring material because it packs down well. But it can be rather slick, dries slowly, and will retain germs and odors. A rock base covered with rock-free clay is an acceptable choice for stalls. It is absorbent, easy on a horse's legs, and provides good drainage. This type of floor is susceptible to pawing, and therefore holes must be filled in.

Wood plank floors, once popular for horse barns, are less common today. This may be due to the high cost of hardwood planks rather than to any other disad-

Synthetic brick floors in aisles are attractive and easy to keep clean.

Although expensive, synthetic brick flooring provides cushioning for horses.

vantages of wood. It is not highly absorbent, and deep bedding must be used to keep stalls dry, to prevent rotting, and to minimize odors. Although wood is easy on a horse's legs, it can be slippery and dangerous.

Concrete stall floors have gained popularity, mainly because concrete is easy to clean and disinfect, is very durable, and can be engineered to provide good drainage. Because of its hardness, concrete must be used in conjunction with some type of thick, soft bedding, such as straw, shredded paper, or wood shavings.

As a flooring material, asphalt is porous and drains well, and is easily cleaned. It is not as hard as concrete, but must still be used in conjunction with a cushioned bedding. Asphalt is cost-effective in most applications, but expensive for small jobs. Its main disadvantage is that it doesn't hold up well. Asphalt can be brittle in cold weather and sticky in hot weather. Once a horse damages a corner of the asphalt surface, the damage usually spreads. An asphalt floor must be repaved every few years.

Today, many horsemen lay rubber mats on top of asphalt and concrete floors to provide cushioning and traction. In addition, some type of bedding is often used on top of the mats.

Some horsemen lay crushed stone on a bed of dirt or concrete and top it off with

Rough-surface concrete has many advantages for aisle floors.

rubber stall mats. This arrangement is easy to clean and sanitize. According to manufacturers of rubber mats, bedding is minimized when mats are used, and the savings can pay for the mats in as little as a year and a half.

Aisleways are commonly constructed of dirt, wood flooring, concrete, or masonry. Dirt aisleways are inexpensive, absorbent, and can be raked clean. But they are almost never level, and if not well drained, can be plagued by puddling and dampness.

Wood flooring is attractive, but expensive. A quality hardwood, such as oak, is necessary due to the heavy traffic that aisleways must bear. Wood floors can be slippery and dangerous, particularly for young or skittish horses. Still, a slip on a wood floor is less likely to injure a horse than a fall on rough concrete and may be considered the best compromise for aisleways.

Brick aisleways are very attractive, although labor costs make them initially expensive. Like wood floors, brick aisleways are slippery when wet. In order to provide adequate drainage, masonry floors must be graded at a slight angle, and drain systems must be engineered into the design. The uneven surface of a masonry floor can cause horses to stumble.

Textured concrete is popular for aisleways. It is easily cleaned, can be sloped for

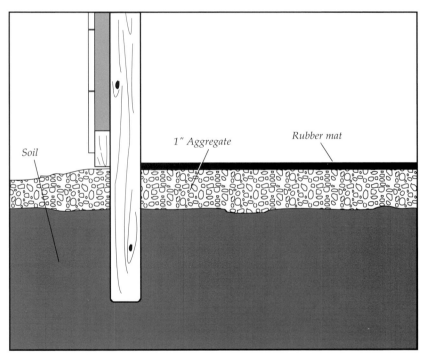

Soil   1" Aggregate   Rubber mat

Improved site pad.

Rubber mats are expensive, but save on bedding.

drainage, and provides good footing. However, the concrete texture can wear smooth over a period of years, and resurfacing may be necessary to ensure safety. One show barn has a concrete floor with a stamped pattern that resembles cobblestone. It is attractive and durable, yet cheaper than a masonry floor.

Should a horse fall on textured concrete, he can sustain cuts and abrasions. One solution is to cover the concrete with artificial turf, preferably a durable fabric that is easily washed clean.

A new floor product is catching on in top breeding barns and race tracks throughout the country. It is a brick made of recycled rubber. The bricks are a high-dollar flooring option, but they offer great safety and excellent traction.

Stall Bedding

Bedding serves to absorb urine, mask manure odor, provide a comfortable place for your horses to lie down, and to relieve pressure on their legs. A clean stall also helps keep your horses cleaner and healthier, and reduces problems with parasites and infection caused by bacteria.

Bedding falls into two categories: absorptive or draining. Various types of straw are all in the draining category, and sawdust, peat moss, paper, and tanbark are absorptive. Wood chips or shavings fall somewhere in the middle.

The type of stall bedding you choose will be influenced by local availability and the type of stall flooring you've chosen. In wood-producing regions, good sawdust and wood shavings may be readily available and inexpensive. In farming regions, straw may be the preferred bedding.

It is important to consider value, because an average 12 by 12-foot stall will

Shavings used in the stall and in the aisle.

require two to four bales of bedding per week. You can save on bedding by investing in rubber stall mats, which cut down on the quantity of bedding needed to cushion hard ground surfaces.

Wood shavings, wood chips, and wood bark can often be purchased at feed stores, but a less expensive alternative is to go directly to furniture manufacturers or lumber mills. Pine shavings are preferable to hardwood shavings, which may contain chemicals that can dry or otherwise injure hoofs. Oak shavings contain tannic acid, which can cause hoofs to heat, making horses uncomfortable. And beware of black walnut shavings; these contain toxins that can lead to founder and death.

Sawdust may be used for bedding, but is more troublesome than wood shavings or chips. Airborne dust can cause respiratory problems and can injure sensitive mucous membranes around the eyes. Sawdust can build up around the frog of a horse's foot, causing irritation and drying. Finally, sawdust can make barn cleaning a bigger chore, clogging drains and settling like mist on tack, equipment, and all flat surfaces. If you must use sawdust, look for a

Sawdust may be used for bedding, but is more troublesome than wood shavings or chips.

47

Chopped paper bedding is very absorbent and spongy.

coarse variety and avoid the fine sawdust produced in the process of finishing wood.

Recycled paper, usually newsprint that has been chopped or shredded, is another option for stall bedding. The supply of newsprint, or sometimes phone directories, is not dependent on the weather or a geographic location.

At present, buying shredded or chopped paper in 1,000-pound bales from a commercial supplier is not a workable solution for most horsemen. Smaller bales of paper are not readily available in many regions.

To chop or shred his own bedding, an individual must first adapt equipment, such as a wood chipper, to do the job.

One study showed that 12.2 pounds of paper bedding is sufficient per day per horse, as compared to 17.9 pounds of straw bedding or 39.5 of wood shavings. Neither straw nor shavings are as absorbent as paper, which means paper bedding becomes soggy quicker. However, paper is biodegradable and weed-free.

Many people prefer the look and smell of shavings over paper bedding. And disposal of paper bedding can be a problem. It can clog up a manure spreader, and looks unsightly if scattered across a field.

Straw—either wheat, oat, or rye—makes a fine bedding and is preferred by many horsemen. It drains moisture well,

and, because it is not highly absorptive, it will not dry the hoofs. Of the different varieties of straw, wheat straw is preferred for its high glaze, which keeps it from becoming over-moist and sloppy. It is also less likely that a horse will eat much wheat straw.

Straw manure has the added attraction of being popular among gardeners. You may be able to put the manure to work for you in the garden, or you may find local gardeners willing to haul off your manure pile, or even pay a modest price for it.

Other products used for bedding include peat moss, pine needles, rice hulls, and even a specially prepared bedding of dried sugar cane. Peat moss is especially desirable for its high absorbency, without

the side effect of drying out hoofs. After being used in the stall, it can be used for gardening. However, peat moss may be hard to get or expensive in many parts of the country.

No matter what type of bedding you choose, avoid dusty materials and keep an eye on your horses to be sure that the bedding materials aren't causing any health problems.

STALLS

Barns may be designed to please people, but stalls should suit horses.

BECAUSE HORSES are positively ingenious in finding ways to hurt themselves, it's important that all stalls be built for safety. Although this may seem obvious to you, the horse person, it may not be to the individual who builds your barn.

I met one woman who contracted a residential home builder to construct her barn. While he built the stalls, she spent most of her day making sure that each nail was driven flush with the board, each board edge was protected from cribbing, and on and on. Long before the job was finished, both of them were angry and upset. The carpenter because he didn't appreciate her building advice, and the woman because she felt the builder was careless about her horses' safety. Had the carpenter known a little more about safe stall construction, a lot of frustration could have been avoided.

Construction and Materials

Different horses have different stall requirements. Generally, miniature horses

A combination of wood and metal grillwork is sturdy and aids ventilation.

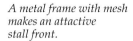
A metal frame with mesh makes an attactive stall front.

get along alright in 8 by 8-foot stalls, and yearlings do okay in 10 by 10-foot box stalls. Mature mares and geldings require 12 by 12-foot stalls, and stallions require stalls 14 to 16 feet long and wide. In all cases, ceiling height should be no less than 8 feet at the lowest point.

In standard building construction, materials layouts are designed in increments of 4 feet. You can minimize material costs by keeping this in mind. Trying to design complicated layouts that combine a variety of stall sizes will require extra time and materials. A better plan is to create removable walls that can be adjusted as needs require. This is easily accomplished with free-standing walls. Walls that support overhead loads, such as loft floors or roof structures, do not offer such flexibility.

An excellent solution for horse owners with changing stall requirements is to build removable partition walls between adjacent stalls. You can accomplish this by using ⅛-inch C-channel irons along the front and back wall panels, and completing the partitions with 2-inch-thick boards that slide or are bolted into the channels. By simply moving the channel irons, you can change the width of the stall to suit your needs. This is especially good for creating foaling stalls. If you have two adjacent 12 by 12-foot box stalls, the center partition can be removed to form a 12 by

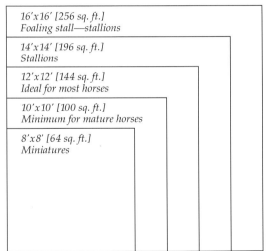

16′x16′ [256 sq. ft.]
Foaling stall—stallions

14′x14′ [196 sq. ft.]
Stallions

12′x12′ [144 sq. ft.]
Ideal for most horses

10′x10′ [100 sq. ft.]
Minimum for mature horses

8′x8′ [64 sq. ft.]
Miniatures

Chart of recommended stall sizes.

24-foot foaling stall adequate for both mare and foal.

Another advantage of using channel irons is that chewed up or broken boards can be easily removed and replaced. If a horse becomes cast against the partition and can't get up, the boards can be removed to allow the animal to get to his feet.

Pipe panels are another easy solution to having removable stall walls.

Channel iron fronts these stalls. Although a horse could stick a leg through, he should be able to pull it out again.

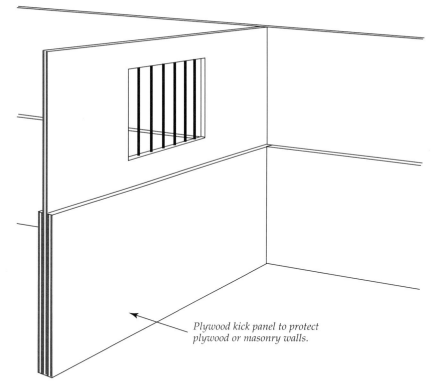

Plywood kick panel to protect plywood or masonry walls.

There are a number of options for building stall walls. The least expensive option is to line the walls with unmilled, rough-sawn (designated RS) or green (uncured) boards that are 2 inches thick. Since the slabs are at least as thick as the nominal dimensions, they are stronger than dry, finished lumber, which is about 1/2 inch smaller than the nominal dimensions. A problem with unmilled lumber is that its rough surfaces splinter easily, which can lead to injuries.

As already mentioned in Chapter 3, a disadvantage of green lumber is that it often warps as it dries, creating problems.

Next up from green lumber in cost and appearance are 2-inch dimensional boards. They are reasonably priced and produce a nice, finished look.

For a truly beautiful look in stall walls, many builders choose 2-inch-thick tongue-and-groove boards. Though expensive, they create an excellent finished look to the stall. Because the boards interlock, they form a very strong wall that is unlikely to be damaged if a horse kicks the boards.

Hardwood boards hold up better than softwoods, and tend to wear more evenly. Oak has the greatest longevity, with hickory, ash, and beech slightly behind. Pinewoods such as Douglas fir and yellow pine are more susceptible to chewing and

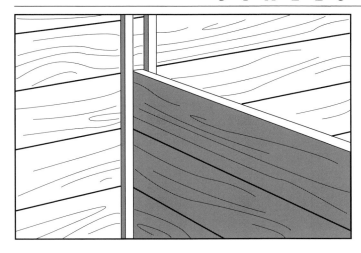 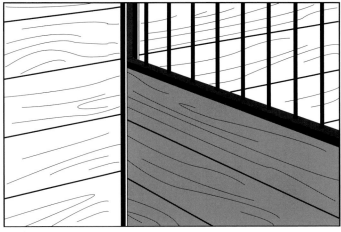

kicking damage. Plywood is often used for stall walls. It must be at least ³/₄-inch thick or it will not stand up to horses' kicks. Generally, if the walls are built of plywood, a second sheet of plywood 4 feet high is placed along each wall to form a kickboard.

Any type of wood stall should be protected from chewing. Wood edges can be protected with metal flashing or strips of gravel shield (1¹/₂ x 1¹/₂ inches or 2 x 1¹/₂ inches) corner metal. These can be purchased at hardware stores or lumber companies. For confirmed chewers, it may be necessary to treat the wood with a non-toxic substance designed to prevent chewing.

Some prefabricated barn builders offer special stall panels that are formed of plywood sandwiched between an outer layer of siding and an inside layer of steel sheet metal. The panel is pushed into a steel framework of L- or T-shaped channels, then bolted in position.

These prefab stall walls are very strong and can withstand a substantial impact. They are clean in appearance, and impervious to cribbing.

If you have decided on building a masonry barn, be aware that the hard walls can damage a horse's hoof if he kicks them. Pawing and other stall vices can also lead to broken hoofs, injured knees and hocks, and skin abrasions. Knowing the stall habits of your horses will help you decide if you need to install kick panels over the masonry. One barn builder suggests using rubber mats like those used for stall flooring to line brick or concrete stall walls.

An important consideration in any stall system is whether to use solid walls or open grill work. Because they are social animals, horses feel more comfortable when they can see their stablemates. Usually, stall fronts are built solid to a height of about 5 feet, with vertical bars running up the open area to the overhead connection.

Walls between stalls are sometimes built solid to avoid fighting or nipping.

But many horsemen opt for a solid wall up to 5 feet, and then vertical bars or pipe panels. Besides creating a more sociable environment, open arrangements provide better air flow throughout the barn. Fully enclosed stalls can trap ammonia from urine and decomposing manure as well as dust, creating an unhealthy situation for any horse.

Perhaps the only situation where solid walls always make sense is for keeping stallions. Some stallions become excited when they can see mares or other stallions. Even so, a stallion stall should still provide good ventilation and natural light, and a view of some sort to prevent cabin-fever. If you feel you must use solid walls, try to design your stall with a back door that opens into an outdoor run and allows the horse to look or go outside.

Although some horsemen do not enclose the tops of their stalls, this can be a dangerous situation. Horses can easily

Perhaps the only situation where solid walls always make sense is for keeping stallions.

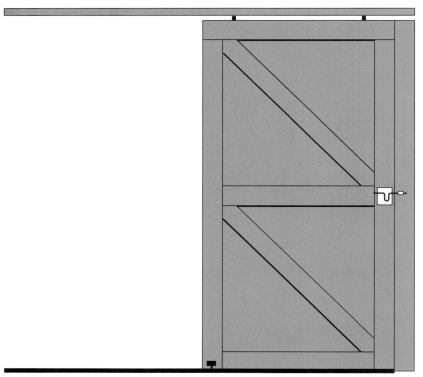

Sliding door.

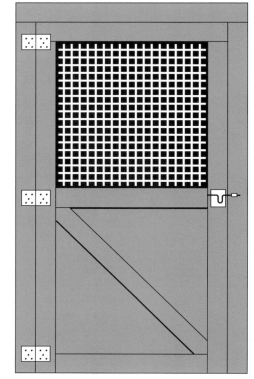

Full door with mesh opening.

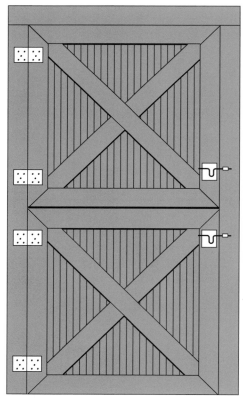

Dutch door.

Bar to prevent damage to Dutch doors.

Traditional Dutch doors allow a horse to be confined without feeling trapped.

jump out of stalls with only 4- or even 5-foot walls. Therefore open stalls can invite tragedy, and the cost of bars, grills, or at least a wire-mesh top is common-sense insurance.

One thing to be certain about is that openings between bars or grills are less than 3 inches. A horse can trap his jaw or hoof (if he rears or kicks) in a wider space, a situation with potentially serious consequences.

Stall Doors

The kind of doors you choose affects safety, ease of service, and aesthetics. All horse doors should be at least 7 feet high and at least 4 feet wide. Doors that open into aisleways should be sliding doors. Swinging doors just take up too much room in aisleways and are unnecessary hazards. The exceptions might be small stables of only a few horses, or stables with extremely wide aisleways.

Most sliding doors are hung on the outside of the stall wall, but they can also be built as hideaways, which slide right into the wall frame. Tracks of heavy steel with nylon runners are standard for sliding doors. Sliding doors should include guides along the bottom that prevent the doors from swinging. Without the guides to hold the door in position, a horse could

push against the door bottom, and might even escape from his stall.

Doors that open onto outdoor aisleways, pastures, or runs afford the horseman greater choices. Dutch doors, which feature separate swinging panels on top and bottom, usually come first to mind for most horsemen. Not only are they attractive, they are practical. During cold weather and stormy days, Dutch doors can be closed tight to seal out drafts.

Dutch doors are handy when it's stall cleaning time because the bottom door can be opened while the stall is cleaned, while the top door keeps the horse in his stall, or outside in his run or pasture area. But don't leave the stall unattended. Many horses have been injured trying to sneak under the top door.

When the horse is cooped up in his stall, the top door can be left open to allow him to watch the world outside. Some horses enjoy this so much that they'll spend their days leaning against the stall door. Eventually, even strong hinges can twist or pull loose from this steady pressure. The hinges may even break, or become damaged to the extent that the door is hard to open.

Some horsemen avoid these problems by installing a removable 2 by 4- or 2 by 6-inch board held by brackets just inside the

Large windows on this Arizona barn encourage air movement.

Attractive stall doors that allow the horse to look out.

bottom door. This prevents damage to the bottom door, while allowing the horse to lean all he wants.

Solid doors with open panels, usually of heavy wire mesh or steel pipe, also allow horses to gaze at the world outside. In cold winter climates, some provision must be made to cover the open panels to prevent drafty stall conditions. In hot climates, a steel or nylon fence gate may be all that's necessary for a stall door.

Although sliding doors will work as outside stall doors, they don't seal well. Drafts are better avoided with Dutch doors or hinged solid doors. However, in situations where the swing-path of the door may be hampered by snow loads, a sliding door may be the best option.

No matter what type of door you choose, or where it is placed, you need to secure it with a strong, horse-proof latch. Horses are magicians at picking latches. Some horses will patiently work at the problem for days on end and will eventually find a way to spring the latch.

If you have a horse who is a known latch-picker, you can install two locks—one at the regular height and another at the base of the door that can be opened and closed with your foot.

The most common latch is the U-shaped horse latch. It is strong and difficult for a horse to open. The only drawback to this bolt-latch design is its protruding end, which could injure a horse who bangs into it. When the door is opened, the bolt must be pulled back to keep the sharp end from

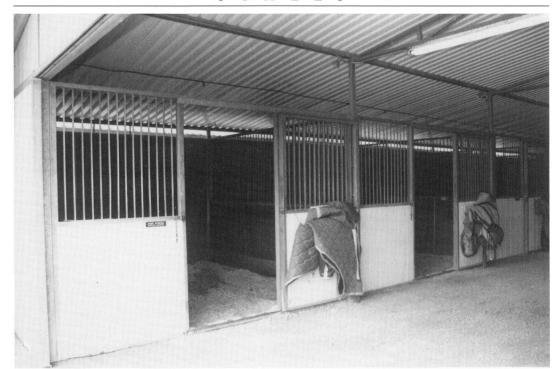

All-metal stalls with sliding doors.

sticking out beyond the door edge. Spring-loaded latches will automatically return the latch bolt to a safe position. Some horsemen recess the latch bolt, or install wood blocks above and below the latch so the horse will strike those instead of the latch itself.

If you need a latch that can be opened from both inside the stall and outside, there is a spring-loaded handle design that works well. It features a heavy bolt similar to the type used on old refrigerator doors, and clicks shut when the door is pulled closed. However, a determined horse can usually puzzle out this particular type of latch.

Incidentally, some stalls with floor-to-ceiling walls can be very difficult, or impossible, for a person to escape from. These stalls should have door latches that can be opened from the inside. Otherwise a person could be trapped in the stall if the door swings shut.

One latch to avoid is the horseshoe latch, a dead-bolt type with a horseshoe welded to the bolt for a handle. Although these latches have visual appeal, many horses have broken jaws caught in the horseshoe. Safer, sturdy latches are not that expensive.

Chain latches work well, as long as the latch is out of reach of the horse. If you have door screens or grills, a simple chain latch will work well. It's best to recess the latches. The protruding nail or rod used to hook the chain can lead to injury.

Stall Furnishings

When outfitting a stall, keep things simple. A hay manger, grain box or tub, and a source of water are the essentials. Some horsemen do not even use hay racks or mangers, preferring to feed hay on the floor or bedding. But this practice wastes feed and can lead to ingestion of sand and dirt, and parasite (worms) infestation picked up from manure. Feeding alfalfa on the floor, bedding, or ground is not a good idea because it usually results in a lot of the leaves being shattered and lost.

For grain, many horsemen use feed buckets or tubs made of rubber or heavy-duty plastic or other synthetic materials. In older barns, a grain box was usually built into one end of a wood manger, but this is seldom done anymore. Building a manger and grain box from lumber requires more time and carpentry skills than does installing a ready-made hay rack and feed tub.

It is common to position hay racks or mangers near the front of the stall, usually in a corner that can be easily reached from the aisleway. Especially handy are the swing-out hay racks built into the front wall. These can greatly simplify feeding.

A small door or opening that is just big enough for a grain scoop can make grain handling simple.

Especially handy are the swing-out hay racks built into the front wall. These can greatly simplify feeding.

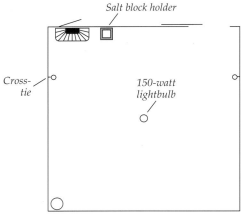

Salt block holder

Cross-tie

150-watt lightbulb

12'x12' stall
Automatic waterer
Sliding door
Easy-access hay rack

12'x12' stall
Bucket waterer
Sliding door [inside]
Dutch doors [outside]
Corner hay rack

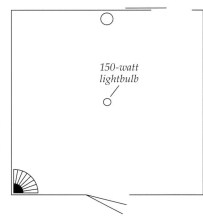

150-watt lightbulb

Common stall floor layouts.

A swing-out door for feeding.

Hay racks are usually made of tubular steel, and may feature a grain trough at the bottom. Aluminum or sheet metal hay racks are also available, but their sharp edges can be hazardous.

The bottom of an overhead hay rack should be about the height of a horse's withers. Hay racks placed higher force the horses to pull down on the hay. Hay dust can filter into nostrils and eyes, a situation that can lead to respiratory difficulties or eye infection. Mounting the rack too low can cause injury if the horse should accidentally catch a hoof in the rack. Racks should be large enough to hold 20 or more pounds of hay. Bars should be spaced about 3 inches apart, because horses may catch and even break their jaws between wider bars.

Ideally, the grain trough at the bottom of the hay rack is big enough to catch hay, especially alfalfa leaves, that fall from the rack. This eliminates a lot of wasted feed, and prevents a horse from ingesting sand or bedding while picking up alfalfa leaves.

Alternatives to hay racks are nylon or rope hay nets. The main advantage to nets is that horses cannot be injured if they should hit or kick them. But if a horse should catch a hoof in a hay net, he can be injured, so make certain to hang them at about the height of the withers.

Another problem with nets is that many horses treat them as toys, and constant chewing and pulling can wear them out rather quickly. Hay nets are also time consuming to fill.

If a hay manger-grain box is built from lumber, installing a piece of sheet metal on

Wall-mounted feeder beside an automatic watering cup.

the bottom of the grain box will make it last much longer. Also, leaving a couple of inches of space between the floor of the manger and side walls makes it easy to sweep chaff and other debris out of the manger. Then, treat all of the edges with an anti-chew preparation, or cover them with sheet metal or dry-wall corner strips.

If you already have wooden mangers, you can increase their life expectancy by treating with an anti-chew product or by lining the edges with metal strips, such as dry wall corner strips. Check the manger each time you feed, and keep a lookout for loose nails or screws, as well as splinters and broken boards.

If the manger is splintered and worn, now may be the time to replace it with a safer hay rack or with rubber feed buckets.

Water

Buckets are the most common and least expensive method of meeting a stabled horse's water needs. Heavy rubber buckets with heavy-duty bails should be hung near the front of the stall in a place that allows easy, twice-daily refilling. Hanging the bucket a few feet from the hay rack or on an opposite wall will help keep the water cleaner. Buckets should hold at least 5 gal-

lons, since a mature horse needs 10 to 12 gallons of water a day. You'll need to check the buckets frequently and refill them at each feeding.

Although plastic or other synthetic buckets are light and easy to handle, they can shatter in cold weather. A rubber bucket can be pounded on with a hammer to get rid of ice.

More and more horsemen are discovering the convenience of automatic waterers. Not only do they provide a constant supply of clean water, many feature heaters that keep the water from freezing and maintain it within the ideal temperature range for horses—between 40 and 75 degrees Fahrenheit.

Most automatic waterers feature a float valve system. As the horse drinks, the valve goes down and a fresh supply of water refills the bowl. Some horses learn to amuse themselves by opening the valve and spilling water into the stall. Some automatic waterers have a screen over the valve so the horse can't play this game.

Heated waterers usually have separate or connected heating units that warm the pipe leading to the bowl. Be certain that any electrical wires connected to the

Most automatic waterers feature a float valve system.

A float-controlled automatic waterer that contains a heating element.

make sure, however, that the horses who share the waterer are compatible, because a bossy horse may try to keep its neighbor from drinking. Furthermore, be aware that a shared waterer or feeding container means shared bacteria, and the opportunity to spread illness and infection.

Although automatic waterers are indeed a time-saver, they also have other disadvantages. As one example, you cannot be sure if a horse is drinking adequately. As another, if you are on a well system and the electrical power goes off for any length of time, your horses will be out of water. (Buckets, on the other hand, hold more water than does the average automatic waterer.)

A more serious problem: Electrically heated automatic waterers are subject to electrical problems. They can be minor, resulting in a horse getting a "buzz" from the waterer, stopping him from drinking; or they can be fatal. For this reason, waterers should be installed by a licensed electrician; and they should be periodically checked. Also, pay attention to your horses. If one is pawing at his waterer, acting thirsty but not drinking, chances are there's a problem with the waterer. Or if he's not eating properly, perhaps it is because he's not drinking and is becoming dehydrated.

Also keep in mind that stock tanks with electric heaters can have the same problems.

In addition to outfitting the stall with a waterer and feeders, you may wish to add a holder for a salt or mineral block. There are wall-mounted holders for blocks or you might put the block on a small platform under the feeder. Some horsemen like to leave a small block in the grain trough. This can keep horses from eating their grain too quickly, because they must push the block around to get to the grain.

One final stall option is a provision for a tie ring. It will be handy when you need to groom a horse or clean his stall. You may also find it handy for restricting a horse from water after exercise.

waterer or the heating unit are covered in rubber conduit tube or run inside a wall and away from the horse's mouth. This will prevent accidental electrocution or injury.

Although some stables have automatic waterers along the back wall of a stall, in most cases it is more economical to install the plumbing in the middle of the barn. In a center aisle design, the main water line runs through the aisle, with faucets or automatic waterers branching off to the stalls on either side.

Some automatic waterers can be situated between stalls to service two horses. This arrangement will save on costs. You should

This loafing shed has dividers so that even the lowest horse on the pecking order can eat. It is also easy and safe to feed the horses because it isn't necessary to get into the corral with them.

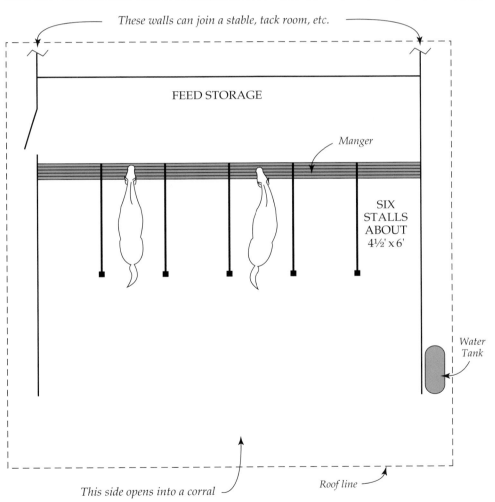

These walls can join a stable, tack room, etc.

FEED STORAGE

Manger

SIX STALLS ABOUT 4½' x 6'

Water Tank

This side opens into a corral

Roof line

CLIMATE CONTROL

Confining horses inside makes us responsible for their environment.

PROBABLY THE foremost reason that people build horse barns is to protect their animals from extreme weather, as well as themselves when they are working with their horses. The proof is that the busy season for barn building is late summer to late fall—just before the onset of winter.

However, many horsemen don't give much thought to the climate stresses that exist *inside* a barn. For example, infectious diseases can spread rapidly in stables where high humidity and lack of adequate ventilation optimize the living conditions for bacteria, fungus, and molds. High urine concentrations in poorly ventilated stalls can cause health problems. Excess heat buildup can lead to heat exhaustion.

Combine these potentially unhealthy conditions with close confinement and it's easy to see why horses kept in stables for large portions of the day are actually more likely to develop respiratory problems and some types of diseases than those left outside. This is why it is important to consider climate control as part of the stable planning process.

Climate is dependent on three factors—temperature, humidity, and air movement. Horses can tolerate a fairly broad temperature range and those horses kept outdoors in subzero weather can get along just fine if they have adequate feed and some type of windbreak. However, studies suggest that horses function most efficiently in temperatures ranging between 40 to 70 degrees and a humidity of between 40 to 60 percent.

In all but the coldest parts of the United States, horse barns do not need heating systems. A sufficiently insulated barn will maintain an inside temperature 10 to 15 or more degrees above the outside temperature. A building with no insulation, however, will have an inside temperature nearly equal to the outside temperature.

In warm and moderate climates, where temperatures seldom drop much below freezing, neither insulation nor heating is necessary.

Because most horses are kept in 12-foot

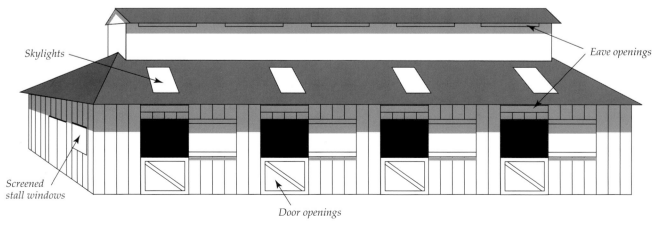

Skylights

Eave openings

Screened stall windows

Door openings

62

box stalls, animal density alone is insufficient to heat a building during prolonged periods of freezing weather. In parts of the country where prolonged cold spells are routine, some form of supplemental heating will probably be necessary. Heating systems may also be desirable for stabled horses who will be exhibited during the winter show season. To maintain the short coats desirable for the show ring, it may be necessary to blanket horses throughout the fall and winter months, as well as confine them in stalls with a consistent minimum temperature of at least 45 degrees.

Lighting also plays an important role in maintaining a short coat, because longer periods of light stimulate the shedding process and forestall hair growth. Note: A flourescent light in a cold barn needs to be fitted with a "cold starter" in order to work properly.

Livestock buildings are classified as either cold housing or warm housing. Cold enclosed housing refers to insulated or non-insulated structures that lack auxiliary heating systems. The inside temperature of these buildings is influenced by outside temperatures. Warm enclosed housing refers to enclosed and tightly insulated buildings designed to maintain a minimum above-freezing temperature regardless of outside temperature, the size of the building, or the number of animals housed.

In deciding whether to install a heating system in your horse barn, you need to consider your objectives as well as the prevailing weather conditions in your area. Unless you live in an extreme northern state such as the Dakotas or Montana, or in the high mountains, you probably can get by without a heating system. This is desirable, because heating creates an unnatural environment for horses, one that is more likely to cause respiratory problems. The exception to this rule is the dedicated professional or amateur show horseman who exhibits the year-round. Even in moderate climates, a heated barn may be a necessity to maintain horses in the desired show condition.

Heating systems commonly used in barns include baseboard electrical units installed along alleyways on the outside of the stalls, forced-air gas heating or oil furnaces supplying heat through ceiling ducts, and electrical heat lamps or infrared lamps mounted above stalls, well beyond the horses' reach. Because of the potential fire danger, heaters should be installed by professionals with experience in heating livestock buildings. Gas, oil, and solid fuel-burning systems must be ventilated to the outside to prevent the buildup of toxic exhaust fumes within the building, and need to be regularly cleaned and maintained.

Insulation may be desirable in either cold or warm enclosed housing. Insulation helps slow down heat flow both into and out of the building. Insulation systems work by trapping pockets of air inside ceilings and walls, or within the materials themselves.

Insulation materials include fiberglass or glass-wool batts or blankets, fill-type insulation such as fiberglass and mineral wool, or rigid insulation such as polystyrene, urethane foam, or compressed wood sheathing.

Unless you use stud wall framing, batts or blankets may be difficult to install in wall spaces. Most are backed with paper or foil and have tabs to be stapled to the studs. The backing forms a vapor barrier that helps prevent condensation buildup inside the barn.

Rigid insulation is commonly used in both post-frame and stud-frame buildings, and may be applied as a nail-bed for siding or as finished interior wall panels. In the case of foam insulation, it may be used to fill wall spaces between the exterior siding and the stall and tack room walls. Foam insulation is applied wet and sets up after a few minutes or hours. It must be applied between rigid inside walls and sealed exterior sheathing.

Humidity can be a problem in any barn.

Ventilation equipment is being installed in this new building. In addition to heating and cooling, good ventilation helps to control condensation, which can contribute to respiratory problems.

When shopping for insulation, you'll learn about R-values. R-values involve resistance to heat loss. For example, a wall lined with 5-inch-thick fiberglass batts will have an R-11 rating. Heat loss will be approximately 11 times slower than if no insulation were present. R-values are the sum of the resistances of insulation, lining and siding surfaces, and air spaces. Check with your builder or building materials supplier for the recommended R-values for barn roofs and ceilings for your area, or see the chart included in this chapter.

Good ventilation helps to keep a barn cool, to dissipate manure and manure odors, and to reduce air humidity. It also restores fresh air in barns, helping the horses maintain good health.

In cold enclosed housing, ventilation is often accomplished through passive ventilation systems, such as eave openings, windows, doorways, ridge vents, or cupolas. Cool air is drawn in through the open windows, doors, or ridge vents. Warm air escapes trough the ridge vents, attic vents, or cupolas, or simply dissipates into the attic area. Temperatures in attics can easily climb 20 degrees or more above the ground-level temperatures. In hot climates, louvered panels, ridge vents, or cupolas may be necessary to control excess heat buildup. Mechanical ventilators, such as thermostat-controlled fans or louver openings, may also be installed in attic walls or as ridge vents to dissipate heat from attic areas.

There are two types of mechanical ventilation systems—pressure systems that force air into the barn, and exhaust systems that draw air out of the barn. For efficient performance, choose a system with a capacity of 100 cubic feet of air flow per minute for every 1,000 pounds of animal weight. This should be adequate for outside temperatures below 60 degrees. During extremely cold weather, only about one-quarter of the capacity will be desired, so a variable capacity system will be necessary.

Humidity can be a problem in any barn. A thousand-pound horse will put about 2 gallons of water into the air each day just by breathing. If that moisture has no place to go, a barn can become damp and clammy. Because warm air holds more water vapor than cool air, a warm barn that is closed off to increase the inside temperature may be quite humid. Even on cold winter days, a small ventilating fan or exhaust fan may be necessary.

Vapor barriers may also be needed to control humidity damage to the structure. Vapor barriers are building materials that prevent moisture from escaping through walls and ceilings. Common vapor barriers include polyethylene plastic, Kraft-backed fiberglass insulation, asphalt roofing paper, and water-sealed paints and finishes.

It is important not to sandwich building materials between two vapor barriers, a situation that traps moisture in walls and ceilings. A single vapor barrier, placed just inside the interior wall sheathing or roofing, is recommended. In very hot locales, such as south Florida, it may be more important to keep humidity out of the barn. Green lumber must be allowed to breathe for at least 6 months before a vapor barrier is applied. Consult with your builder or building supplier to determine what type of vapor-barrier system works best with the type of barn you are building.

The cupola is more than decorative. Warm air rises inside the building and is let out through the cupola.

LIGHTS AND WIRING

Plenty of light will benefit both horses and people.

PLANNING FOR electrical needs will make barn work and grooming chores easier and more efficient. Consider all of the various needs you may have for electricity—grooming clippers and vacuums, perhaps a refrigerator for storing medications and refreshments, lighting, heating, a water heater, and perhaps a microwave or hot plate for heating water for mashes or for brewing coffee. In cold-weather barns it may be necessary to heat-tape water pipes and automatic waterers.

In a center-aisle barn, and in some other designs, outlets are usually mounted on the posts that separate a pair of stalls; a reason-able layout is to place one dual or quad outlet for each cluster of four stalls. Interior and exterior electrical outlets should have spring-loaded covers that snap shut when not in use. These prevent hay-dust explosions, and a horse can lick them without being shocked and possibly electrocuted.

When possible, wiring should be routed behind walls, underground, or in conduit. Conduit, either hard rubber or metal, should be used to prevent horses or rodents from chewing through the wire—a primary cause of barn fires.

For safety, you should have a ground-fault interrupter in your barn. These de-

Lots of overhead lights serve both aisle and stalls.

A bubble skylight installed in an asphalt-shingled roof.

vices sense breaks in circuit continuity, such as when an appliance falls into a water basin or a horse chews through a wire. These types of situations instantaneously break the electrical current in the wire.

It is also safer to install the electrical system on a separate circuit from the one used to supply electricity to the home, as well as to have a separate fuse box in the stable. If you use a well pump to supply water, it should have its own breaker switch as well. If a fire should break out and the electrical system is jeopardized, the well will continue to supply water for fire fighting.

Some building codes allow electrical wiring to be run into a building in the same trench as plumbing; others specify separate trenches for electrical and plumbing. Of course, it's usually less expensive to run power into a barn with overhead lines. Your electrical contractor should be aware of the local codes, or you can check with the local building authority.

Horses seem to enjoy lots of light, and they like to be able to see their stablemates. Physiologists at Cornell University's College of Veterinary Medicine discovered that horses allowed to control their own lighting will work to increase illumination levels.

The horses used in the study would turn on lights at all hours of the day and night, and particularly in the early morning hours.

Since horses seemingly prefer lots of light, lighting should be a combination of both electrical and natural lighting. During daylight hours, open doors, windows, and wall panels will help prevent boredom that can lead to stall vices. The sun is also a source of vitamin D, and some sunlight in the barn can help provide this nutrient when the horses cannot be allowed outdoors.

Stall doors that open into outside runs, stall windows, panel openings, and skylights are various means to brighten a barn interior.

Stall windows should be built at least 5 feet from the ground, and covered with heavy mesh screens or bars to prevent horse injuries or window breakage. Windows that open outward at the top and that can be tightly sealed are preferable.

Natural lighting alone probably won't be adequate for all your lighting needs.

We are showing this picture again to depict the overhead hanging lights being installed in this new barn. Switches and outlets are visible on the studs at right.

Metal conduit leads wires into the breaker box, which is fed with a supply cable coming up through PVC pipe.

In hotter climates, good lights extend the usefulness of the arena into the cooler evening hours.

In warm and moderate climates, you may wish to have openings at the top of the stall walls to aid in ventilation and add some light. If snowstorms are a problem, these openings may be closed in winter with translucent fiberglass panels that will allow light in, but keep snow out. Monitor roofs permit a similar arrangement below the eaves of the central roof pitch. In warm climates, open-eaved monitor designs are quite popular.

Skylights, either translucent panels or molded Plexiglas bubbles, can really help brighten a barn's interior. Careful installation is necessary to prevent them from leaking.

Natural lighting alone probably won't be adequate for all your lighting needs, but it will help keep down electricity costs during the day. At night, a stall can be illuminated with a single incandescent light in the middle of the stall. The bulb and fixture should be at least 8 feet from the stall floor and protected by a heavy glass bulb cover or a wire cage.

Aisleways with ceilings lower than 16 feet can be lit with incandescent bulbs or fluorescent lighting. Mercury vapor lights work well for ceilings above 16 feet, and are commonly used for arena lighting. Although initially costly, they produce a higher intensity light with less electricity than incandescent lighting. Fluorescent lighting diffuses too quickly to be effective under high ceilings or to illuminate large areas.

For safety's sake, all wiring should be installed by a licensed electrician.

PLUMBING

9

Convenience should be your primary concern in planning.

LOTS OF WATER outlets make barn cleaning, grooming, and watering chores much easier. If pipe freezing is likely to be a problem, you'll need frost-free hydrants instead of regular water spigots. If you're able to afford a wash rack, you may want to plan on installing a water heater.

If you choose to run electrical power into your barn underground, it's safer to have separate trenches for the wiring and water pipes. Building codes might require it anyway. Though it may be cheaper to run a single trench, you might regret it if a water line breaks and the electrical line

has to be torn up, too.

In cold climates, water pipes need to be buried at least a foot below the frost line. Generally, a depth of 5 feet is adequate to protect water lines from freezing. But 6 feet may be better. It is advisable to route water pipes through low traffic areas and avoid running them under driveways and parking areas. Heavy vehicles can damage even deeply buried water lines. Also, weight will drive the frost deeper in the ground, which may cause pipes to freeze.

In extremely cold climates where freezing is a threat inside the barn, water lines

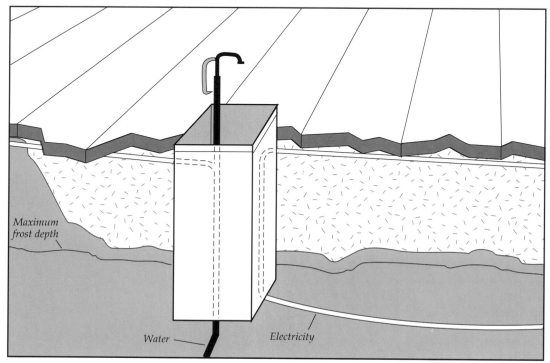

Maximum frost depth

Water —

Electricity

Pipe chase.

Some automatic waterers contain heating elements. This one shares a water supply line with another unit in the adjacent stall.

Corner-mounted automatic unit, with the supply line coming in from the top.

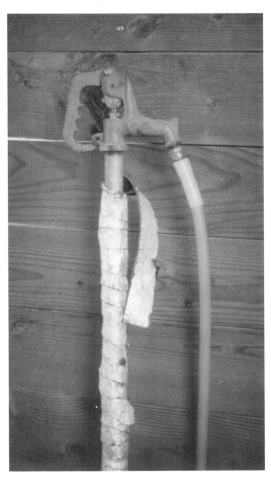

Wrap-around insulating tape protects pipes from freezing.

can be brought into the building through an insulated pipe chase. A simple pipe chase would consist of a square box built of treated lumber that extends below the frost line. The water pipes run up through the chase into the barn. A few wraps of electric heat tape will keep the water from freezing in the pipe. A pipe chase is probably not necessary in warm and moderate climates, or in a heated barn.

Because a horse needs 12 or more gallons of water a day, watering is a big chore if you have more than a couple of horses, especially if the water hydrant is far from the farthest stall. If you keep more than six horses in a barn, you may want to install water hydrants between each cluster of three or four stalls. Generally, you can get by with just one outlet for any barn smaller than six stalls.

Water hoses tend to be inconvenient. After a few months of rolling and unrolling them each time you water, you may wish you had planned more spigots. Hoses also tend to freeze in winter if they are not drained, and if you have to wait for them to thaw, watering your horses can come to resemble a fireman's bucket brigade. A better solution might be automatic waterers.

It's fair to say that automatic waterers are the envy of many horsemen who have to carry heavy buckets. As discussed previously, automatic waterers make clean, fresh water available to horses at all times and will save a lot of labor. Their only drawbacks are that they can freeze in cold weather, they can run over and flood stalls when not correctly adjusted, and they

Large horse facilities place water tanks to serve several enclosures.

When this arrangement is hooked up, the hose comes through the fence via the plastic pipe, then threads into the top of the float valve clamped to the side of the tank.

don't allow the horseman to monitor his horses' water intake.

Look for waterers with some type of heating system if you live in a cold climate. Check the waterers daily to make sure they aren't leaking and that they are supplying water. Finally, have your plumbing installed so that you can shut off individual waterers should you need to deprive a horse of water, such as after a hard workout, or if a stall is not being used.

It's handy to have at least one faucet outside the barn for cleaning trailers and barn equipment or for washing your horse on a warm summer day. Other likely places where water may be desired include tack rooms, lounges, restrooms, and wash rooms. Make certain that your plumbing plans include adequate drainage systems, either leach fields or tie-ins to existing septic systems. There may be building codes or sanitation requirements for the disposal of waste water. Checking with the local building authority before installing a waste water system will help prevent costly mistakes.

Here's one way to install a heater in a water tank. To prevent horses from chewing on it, the electric cord has been run through PVC pipe until it drops through the hole in the plywood. The plywood lid has been treated with an anti-chew product, and is wired down, as is the pipe. The lid keeps the horses from playing with the heater. PVC pipe is sold at building supply centers, and is easy to cut with a regular handsaw. Horses can be killed by chewing on electrical cords.

This automatic waterer in a fence line serves two outside pens.

STORAGE AND WASH AREA

Storage spaces and wash areas are finishing touches to housing for horses.

FOR MOST horsemen, a stable would be incomplete without some provision for storing tack and feed. If you have only a few horses, a corner of the garage may suffice, at least for a while.

But the convenience of storing your equipment in a handy and secure room in the barn will soon have you dreaming of a well-equipped tack room. Feed bags, hay bales, and bedding may soon prevent you from parking your car. And what will you do if your horse habit grows? For all but the most modest horse outfit, a tack room and feed room are necessities.

Tack rooms needn't be large or elaborate. The key to a usable tack room is organization. Even large commercial stables sometimes have what seem to be impossibly small tack rooms, sometimes no larger than a regular stall. For the most part, though, these tack rooms are strictly for the boarders' essential equipment—a saddle, saddle blanket, halter, headstall, and perhaps a grooming kit. For the home horse owners, tack rooms are asked to do

double or triple duty, serving as repositories for barn equipment, grain bins, horse blankets, veterinary supplies, ribbons, trophies, and horse books and magazines. For this reason, it's best to provide ample space for essential equipment, as well as all the associated paraphernalia of horse ownership.

Ideally, a tack room should be well-lit and tightly sealed to keep out dust. Since barn theft is all too common today, a locking door can keep would-be saddle thieves away from your valuable gear. If you have a small stable without a tack room, you may wish to build a large, permanent, lockable chest in an out-of-the-way place.

Saddles take up a lot of room, and you'll want to store them high and dry. Wall-mounted saddle racks, particularly the kind that fold up flat when not in use, are handy for keeping saddles in good condition. In fact, they help maintain the saddle shape, and might keep latigos, stirrup leathers, and cinches

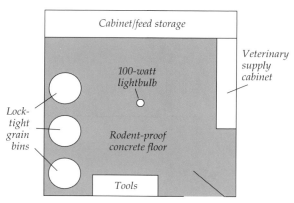

Common feed room layout.

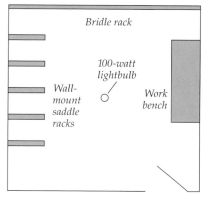

Common 12'x12' tack room.

74

away from gnawing rodents.

Another possibility is a free-standing saddle rack. These are made commercially, or if you're handy, you can build your own. The best have a shelf for storing grooming equipment under the saddle and a keeper to hold a bridle. Metal or plastic 55-gallon barrels make good saddle racks. Just bolt them to a sturdy stud or post on the wall, facing the open end out as handy storage for grooming tools and other tack.

Horsemen have a way of acquiring bits and bridles. We collect bridles for every-day riding, training, and showing. You may find it handy to have special bridle hangers. You can purchase many kinds, including some that are very decorative. But they can be as plain as tuna fish cans nailed to the wall. The natural curve of the can helps keep the bridle in the right shape. Another economical method is 2-inch-thick slices of tree limb nailed to the wall. At some stables, a horse's name is labeled on each bridle holder, ensuring that the right bridle is used on the right horse.

If you blanket your horses, you already know how much space these bulky items can take up in a crowded tack room. This is particularly true when you need to air them out or dry them after a rain. Even

Stacked saddle racks help maximize tack room capacity.

Large chest freezers make great tack storage containers.

A blanket bar and boxes provide storage at the stall entrance.

nylon or Cordura blankets can mold and mildew if put away wet. Some type of rack where blankets can be aired and dried is necessary. Sometimes blankets are left on the racks, or they may be folded and put away when dry. You can buy racks that are free-standing or that are made to be fastened to a wall.

Large chest freezers make great tack storage containers. Blankets, leg wraps, bell boots, show saddle pads . . . almost anything can be stored in them. Often, you can find a non-working freezer in the want ads. But be cautious: Children have been trapped and suffocated in old refrigerators and freezers. Have the freezer lock mechanism removed and install a padlock and hasp. Keep the box locked and warn children never to play in it.

People active in horse shows may prefer to store tack and grooming tools in a tack trunk. A trunk can be roomy enough for a saddle, bridles, a saddle pad, and grooming accessories. By storing all show equipment in a trunk, the horseman can devote himself to other things, knowing that all necessary items are in one place, ready to go.

Another handy tack room feature is a cabinet for veterinary supplies or medicine, leather care supplies, and assorted small items.

For convenience, it's best to plan your tack room near the grooming area. For instance, position the tack room directly across the aisle from the wash room and rack. A non-slip, brushed concrete pad with a drain on the wash rack can also serve as the floor for the tack room.

Stable tools are usually stored in the tack room or feed room. In larger stables there may be a separate storage room or closet for stable tools, although this isn't really necessary. The basic stable tools include a flat shovel, hay fork, manure fork, rakes, broom, and a manure cart or wheelbarrow for cleaning stalls. Tools for repair work include fence pliers, a screwdriver set, hammer and nails and staples, a wire cutter, and miscellaneous hardware such as spare hinges, latches, wire, etc.

Long-handled tools such as rakes, shovels, and brooms can hang on hooks on an out-of-the-way wall in the tack room, feed room, or aisleway. Just make sure that they will not be a hazard close to grooming areas and high-traffic zones.

We all know people whose horses got into stored grain. Sometimes they consume lethal amounts of grain, which usually results in severe founder. It's important to store grain in a tight, dry container

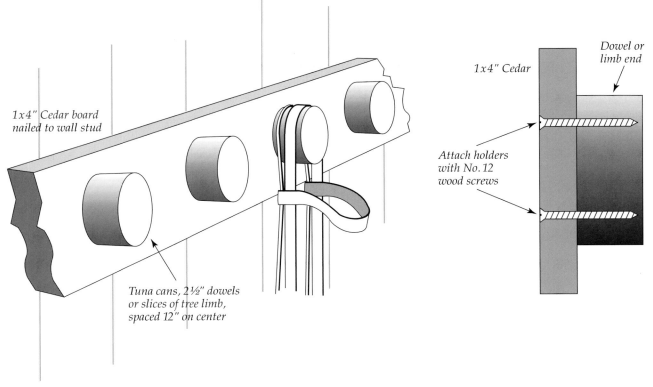

1x4" Cedar board nailed to wall stud

1x4" Cedar

Dowel or limb end

Attach holders with No. 12 wood screws

Tuna cans, 2½" dowels or slices of tree limb, spaced 12" on center

A simple bridle rack.

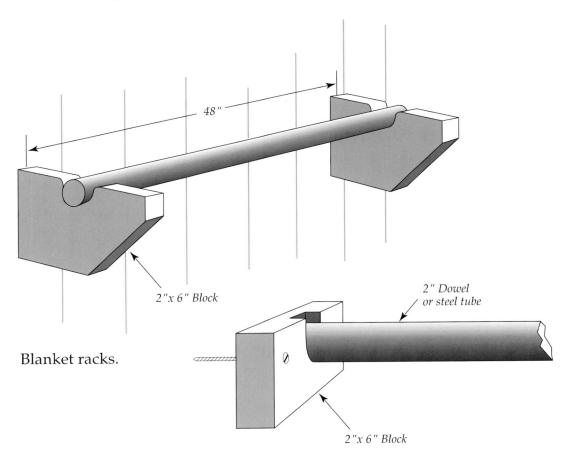

48"

2"x 6" Block

Blanket racks.

2" Dowel or steel tube

2"x 6" Block

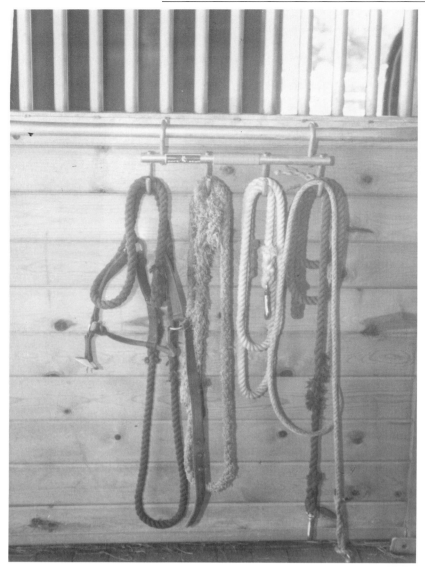

Multiple or single hangers provide a way to keep halters and lead ropes handy.

away from your horses. Many owners use trash cans in the tack room or in an aisleway. If you must keep grain in an aisleway, it's advisable to invest in a container with a lock-tight lid that won't come off even when the container is tipped over. A 30-gallon, locking trash can or feed container can hold up to 100 pounds of grain.

Ideally, it's safest to store grain in a separate room that will keep horses out. An empty stall makes a good feed storage room, provided it can be locked shut.

Besides attracting horses, grain also attracts rodents. If you can afford it, a concrete floor will help keep these pests from raiding the grain supply.

For large horse farms, it is economical to buy grain in bulk. Many big farms have bulk tanks or rodent-proof grain storage rooms, often lined with sheet metal. Deliveries are made directly from trucks through a large door on an outside wall of the building.

For the small stable owner, the economy of buying in bulk may be attractive. Generally, though, it isn't advisable to buy more than a month's supply of grain at a time. Because of their high moisture content, some grains and mixed feeds spoil quickly. Sweet feeds that contain molasses have a particularly short storage life.

Most of us think of molds as a problem in hot, humid conditions, but some, such as fusarium molds that cause moldy-corn (aflatoxin) poisoning in horses, can thrive in

Tractor, trailer, and bulk alfalfa cubes under one roof.

Bulk grain bins are sometimes equipped with an auger to move grain inside.

Bulk shavings can be delivered by the truckload, used by the cartload.

A storage bin for shavings.

near-freezing temperatures. So buy only as much corn or mixed feeds as you will feed in a month. Plain oats, of course, will keep indefinitely if protected from moisture.

Although many people still store hay in their horse barns, the practice is dangerous. Improperly cured hay is prone to spontaneous combustion. A small electrical short or a careless cigarette is all it takes to ignite hay and destroy a barn and everything in it. The best fire protection measure you can employ is a separate storage shelter for your hay and bedding. Don't keep more than a few days' supply of hay and bedding in the barn with your animals.

A wash room in a barn is a luxury for most people. Even committed showmen sometimes rely on wash racks at the show grounds to ready their horses for the ring. Others just tie their horses outside and use a garden hose for washing.

The main advantage of an indoor wash room is its convenience. In mild weather, you can wash at any time of the day or night . . . and even in chilly weather if you have a heated area where the horse can dry thoroughly. A wash area is also handy for treating those foot and leg injuries that require soaking in hot water, or a steady stream of cold water. You will really appreciate this convenience in cold weather! A wash room also means not having to stand in a mud puddle outside, and it facilitates keeping shampoos, conditioners, etc., organized and in one place.

A 12 by 12-foot wash room is a size that fits into most horse barn layouts. You will need a larger area if you plan to wash more than one horse at a time. The walls should be sealed against water damage, or constructed of materials impervious to water. Many rooms are made of concrete blocks. Other possibilities are tile, sheet metal panels, or treated lumber.

The wash room should have a non-slip floor that slopes to a drain. Textured concrete floors work well, as do rubber mats laid over concrete or a bed of crushed rock. A perforated drain pipe placed in a trench under the rock bed and tied into a leach field or septic system will help keep the wash room area well-drained. Make sure the mats will not be slippery when wet.

A wash room needs something to

Wall-mounted spool keeps hose out of the way.

which a horse can be tied. The safest is simply a tie ring securely installed in the wall. Although some wash rooms have cross-ties, many veterinarians do not recommend their use because if a horse throws a fit, for whatever reason, he's more apt to be injured than if he's tied with a single lead rope.

A wash room or area can also have a set of stocks installed. They make it easier to wash a fidgety horse, and they can also be used for doctoring, preg-checking mares, etc. Stocks are available commercially, or can be built to specifications. The standard dimension for a set of stocks is about 6 feet long, 28 inches wide, and each side bar about 3 feet above the floor.

One word of caution. If a horse has never been washed before, do not tie him hard and fast, or put him in stocks, and

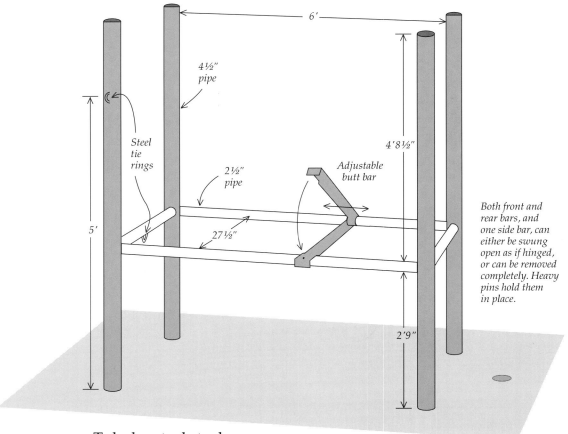

6'

4½"
pipe

Steel
tie
rings

2½"
pipe

Adjustable
butt bar

27½"

4'8½"

Both front and
rear bars, and
one side bar, can
either be swung
open as if hinged,
or can be removed
completely. Heavy
pins hold them
in place.

5'

2'9"

Tubular steel stocks.

Wash area with traction mats and sturdy tie-rail on the perimeter.

turn the hose on him full force. Proceed slowly and let him get gradually accustomed to this new experience . . . especially if he's standing on concrete.

To complete the wash room, include a shelf or plastic rack for storing shampoo and grooming tools. A few rubber curry combs, brushes, some towels, and a sweat scraper are the essential tools.

Warm water grooming is more pleasant than cold water alone, and is a must in very cold weather. If you live in a moderate or cold climate, your wash room plumbing should include a 30-gallon water heater that can be shut off with a switch when it is not needed. If you live in a warm climate, you may not need the heater at all. Some folks in southern states find it cheaper and easier to build a wash rack outdoors instead of building an elaborate and costly wash room.

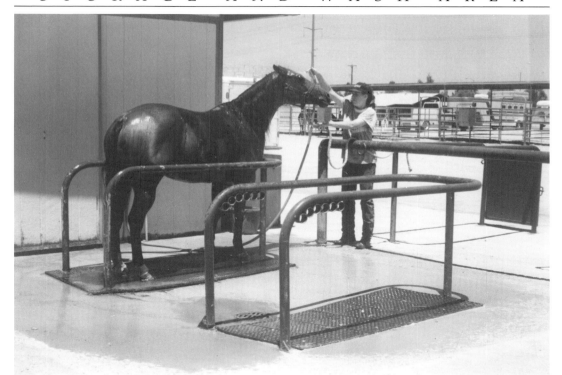

Pipe stocks make washing easier. Note no-skid footing.

Center tie-rail services four wash stocks. Two drains serve the whole area.

PENS, CORRALS, AND PASTURES

Your horse won't spend all his time under a roof.

IT IS AMAZING how people often hurry to complete horse barns and other out-buildings without giving thought to completing turn-out areas such as pens, corrals, and to fencing pastures. After building a number of barns, I began to notice a pattern of new home buyers who had barns built before they thought about how they would handle exercise and turn-out areas.

One couple had their barn built, and, on move-in day, they brought in five horses and a miniature pony from their previous home. There were no pens or fenced areas on the property, and after a few days, the bored horses started eating the barn.

To save his new barn, the owner put up a single, small electric-fence corral on one side of the barn. The next morning, he turned the horses out for the day and left. He came home to pandemonium. A colt and the pony had been kicked and bitten by an aggressive mare. A few of the posts that supported the barn overhang were chewed up, and one horse had cut himself on a steel T-post.

It took nearly 2 weeks to get a fence crew to erect some proper pens and a perimeter fence to give the horses more room. In the meantime, the horses and the barn suffered more injuries.

Although buyers of developed horse properties usually find fencing in place, some new home buyers and those starting from scratch are faced with the choice of

This attractive fence is not sturdy enough to work well in a smaller enclo-sure. Post-and-rail fences also have a shorter life span than other fencing.

Pipe is used to fence runs on this Oklahoma farm.

building fences first or spending their savings on a barn.

Ideally, barns, pasture fences, corrals, and pens should all be built in conjunction with one another. But if this doesn't fit into your budget, it's often better to take care of the fencing first, and attend to the building later.

A few pens, an exercise area, and an arena will benefit your horses more than a fully equipped stable with no turn-out facilities. A few simple and inexpensive sheds can serve as shelter until the budget allows for a full-fledged barn.

Keep in mind that horses, by nature, are outdoor animals. Given the choice of being in a barn stall or outside in a stall run or small pasture, a horse will spend about 90 percent of his time outdoors.

Even if it's not feasible to fence your property before the barn is built, it's best to plan and follow through with building at least minimal turnout and exercise facilities right from the start.

Before looking at the various fencing options, it's useful to get a handle on the types of enclosures found on horse farms. First, we should recognize that there's little consistency in the terms used to describe various enclosures.

A stall pen may also be called a stall run; a small pasture may be called a paddock, especially in the eastern United States, or a trap, in some ranching areas, especially Texas. One rancher, when asked how big a corral was, responded, "It depends on how many horses are in it." A 5-acre pasture with 200 horses would be a corral; a 60-foot round pen with 5 horses in it might also be called a corral.

For the sake of clarity, I've set standards for types of enclosures. These aren't hard and fast, so if you want to call a stall pen a stall run, a small pasture a paddock, or an arena a corral, that's your privilege.

A small pasture is an enclosure ranging from a half-acre to 5 acres in size. These are suitable as free exercise areas for one to five horses, but are generally too small to provide feed without supplementation.

The smaller the enclosure, the more stress on the fencing.

Pipe forms these stall runs for young horses.

Pipe and wire are combined for this fence and gate.

Treated bridge timber was used for this traditional fence and gate on a Wyoming ranch.

A pasture is any larger acreage that, if properly managed, will provide feed for a band of horses.

Strictly speaking, a pen is a small enclosure slightly larger than a stall—roughly 12 by 20 feet. Horses kept in pens, just like horses kept in stalls, must be exercised daily. In my mind, a pen is usually for containing a single horse, or a mare and her foal. Pens are also handy as a means of confining sick or injured horses, those awaiting a farrier, or for limiting the time horses spend on pasture.

Generally, the strongest and safest fencing for a pen is welded tubular steel pipe or prefabricated tubular or square-tube steel panels. When painted, they look good with any barn.

Other possibilities for pens include wire mesh, vinyl board, or wood planks. All of these fence types can be augmented with an electric strand top, bottom, or chest-high. Because they are small, pens and runs must be especially safe and strong. A height of 5 feet is good for geldings, mares, and foals; 7 feet is good for stallions.

For board fences, four or five boards should be used. For pipe fencing, at least five pipes, a foot apart, are best. A horse who can't reach his head through will not push on a fence as much, won't fight with neighboring animals, and won't rub his mane out.

When confining small foals, it's best to use something to close off the space at the bottom of your fencing. They lie down so much that they are prone to get their legs

This synthetic fencing makes an attrractive arena fence.

Large painted pipe on top and smaller diameter pipe below are used to contain mares and foals.

Low troughs mean less wasted feed. Setting the troughs out away from the fence allows timid horses to eat without being harassed.

Pasture feeders made from big tires are great for feeding groups of horses.

In southern climates, horses just need shade. Feeders and waterers are mounted on the fence panels.

A canopy offers shade and protects the feeder from rain.

Movable hay feeders for supplemental feeding in pasture.

caught under a bottom rail or board, or even roll under a fence.

For mature horses, the bottom of the fence should be about 2 feet off the ground. Anything lower will tend to trap and injure legs of horses lying down or rolling.

A run is large enough for a horse to move around, exercise freely, trot some, and even lope. Although it may be only 20 feet wide, a run can be between 75 and 200 feet long, and closer to 200 if you want your horses to really stretch their legs.

Corrals are large pens, whether round or rectangular, that are used for holding horses and other livestock. Special-use corrals, such as round pens, are often used for training.

Aside from the special uses, corrals usually hold a number of horses. And horses have a pecking order that is magnified when a group is compressed into a small space. The order is determined and enforced by kicks, bites, and threatening gestures.

Because of the pushing and fighting that can take place in a corral, a strong, safe structure is necessary. Gates should be strong and have heavy, horse-proof latches. But the buyer must avoid protruding latch pieces that can cause injury. Gates should be a minimum of 4 feet wide to pre-

vent hip and shoulder injuries. Pipe gates seem to hold up better and are lighter than wood gates. Keep in mind that a metal or aluminum-slat gate can cause major injuries if a horse gets a leg through it.

If horses are fed and watered in corrals, fighting is more of a problem. Feeders should be spaced to allow room for the pecking order to operate. Feeders should be accessible from all sides, should have no sharp edges, and should be located away from gates. Fence-mounted buckets or hay racks can be used if they are spread out. Rubber feeders are safest.

Grain troughs can be used to feed a number of horses. One that is away from a fence is best. But free-standing troughs should have a base that is narrower than the feed area, to prevent leg injuries. It may help to build partitions

Groups of mares and foals require room for the pecking order to operate smoothly.

Paddocks and pastures fenced with pipe and cable are attractive and low-maintenance.

The only drawback to
this type of fence is that
a horse could possibly
hang a hoof or shoe in it.

Traditional white plank
fencing is attractive but
expensive and requires
maintenance.

93

along a trough to separate horses. This will prevent one dominant horse from scaring off the rest.

Another possibility for grain is feed bags. These assure that each horse gets the intended amount of grain. But be sure to take them off promptly—horses have drowned from sticking their noses into a tank while wearing a feed bag.

Galvanized steel or aluminum tanks were the most common way to water stock for years. But they can rust or leak after a few years, and many are gradually being replaced by tanks made of synthetic materials. These are easier to clean and move, and last much longer.

Many horse farms install automatic waterers in pens and pastures. Although they are a convenience, they should be checked regularly to make sure they are working.

Discarded bathtubs are sometimes used as waterers. But their cast-iron edges can be dangerous and cause many leg injuries. A wooden frame around the tub can prevent most injuries.

In cold climates, an electric stock tank heater may be a wise investment. It not only saves the work of breaking ice, it protects the health of your horses by encouraging them to drink more water than they would without one. Heaters can be free-floating (a protective cage is needed for heaters used in synthetic tanks) or attached to the tank wall. The conventional heaters produce low-intensity heat, usually from a copper element, that is enough to keep water from freezing.

Tank heaters have been known to short-circuit and electrocute a horse. In most cases, the electrical cords leading to the heater are encased in a metal coil to keep horses from chewing on them. Look for tank heaters that are the right capacity for your tank, and that have a guarantee or a safety certification.

One other warning about tank heaters: After enjoying the first month without battling ice, you may get another kind of shock when you open your electric bill. Running a heater full time will also heat up your bill.

One alternative to heaters is an insulated pasture waterer. These come in several sizes and configurations, but basically operate on the same principle as the Thermos bottle. An inner tank holds water, and is insulated from the cold by a vacuum-sealed outer container. Some models have float valves to keep the water level standard, and others require filling.

If pastured horses get their water from a windmill tank, check it frequently to make sure it's working properly. If a pipe or rod breaks, no water will be pumped, even if the windmill continues to rotate.

Board and V-mesh fence is hard to beat.

ROUND PENS AND ARENAS

These enclosures are for training, exercise, and competition.

Breaking Pens and Round Pens

Round pens are high on most horsemen's wish lists. They are useful for training horses of any age.

A breaking pen is a small round pen, usually between 30 and 50 feet in diameter. These pens are useful for training young horses in ground aspects such as leading, sacking out, hobbling, saddling, and for first rides.

Many trainers believe that a breaking pen should have solid walls somewhere around 7 feet high. The theory is that such an enclosure makes the horse focus his full attention on the trainer. With no outside distractions or view of a possible escape, the unbroke horse is forced to pay attention to the human. Although a young horse will not be tempted to try scaling a solid wall, the human doesn't have a means of escape, either. This can be a problem if the horse decides to fight. Another problem with solid-wall pens is the lack of air movement in hot weather, and reduced sunshine to dry them out after rain or snow.

For these and other reasons, some trainers prefer a breaking pen with open space in the walls. They maintain that a young horse will have to deal with distractions eventually, and that it's better

The large arena in the foreground is used for exercise and training. The high-walled round pen behind it is used primarily for training, especially of young horses.

T-Cross Ranch near Colorado Springs has a 150-foot-diameter round pen. The post in the center supports a sprinkler, fed by an underground water line. A round pen of this size is popular with cutting horse trainers.

to start out with them right away. One disadvantage of walls with spaces is that a rider might catch a foot between boards. There is also a danger of a frantic horse trying to climb a wall and sticking a leg through.

A good compromise is walls that are solid for the bottom 3 or 4 feet. Some trainers line the lower half of the corral wall with rubber conveyor belting.

Some basic horse psychology applies to any style of breaking pen. Horses have a clearly defined personal space. When a person approaches to within 15 to 20 feet of an unbroke horse, the animal's instincts tell him to flee. In a breaking pen, the horse has nowhere to go. So the trainer uses this instinct to control the horse. By advancing a few steps, he applies pressure. If the horse reacts correctly—facing the trainer rather than turning tail and threatening to kick, for example—the trainer can move back a few steps and take the pressure off. In this way, the breaking pen can serve as a tool to develop trust.

Although a small round pen is invaluable for working with unbroke horses, it has limits. Most breaking pens are too confined for any serious riding. Because the horse must constantly turn in a tight circle, he can easily strain muscles and tendons. And the real small pens don't work well for longeing and driving.

Much of a horse's schooling usually takes place in a larger round pen. And a good-size round pen is a useful training tool for any saddle horse. A full-size round pen—often 60 to 70 feet in diameter—is big enough to allow the horse to canter without causing him undue strain. Cut-

ting horse trainers sometimes work horses in round pens as large as 160 feet in diameter, but these are basically arenas.

Unless you regularly handle a number of unbroke horses, a small breaking pen is probably a luxury. Most of a young horse's basic training can be carried out in the large round pen, and the more advanced training can continue there.

A good round pen must be stout. You might use prefab steel fence sections, or build the pen of welded pipe. A height of 5 feet is good for most horses, but 7 feet would be better for unbroke horses.

For safety, it's wise to slope the walls of the round pen outward at the top. This helps protect the rider's knees and legs if the horse crowds the wall.

One of the better round pens I've seen is at the U.S. Air Force Academy riding stable near Colorado Springs. The pen is 64 feet in diameter and the sides are 4 feet tall.

Boarders and members of the Academy Equestrian Team use this round pen every day as a training and turnout facility. It was built with economy and durability in mind, and serves as a good model for the average horseman. I'd like to describe how it was built, so that, with a few changes, you have an example of how you can complete your own, expensive round pen.

The round pen at the U.S. Air Force Academy near Colorado Springs is 64 feet in diameter.

The diameter will define the use of the round pen.

A first suggestion: If you plan to work with unbroke horses, you may want to build a higher wall. A 5- or 6-foot wall would be better for green horses, and would also keep horses from putting their heads over it.

If you wish to build a higher pen based on this design, use longer posts and incorporate more rails at the top.

The base for the Academy pen is a 64-foot diameter circle that is depressed 8 inches below the surrounding terrain. Edges are angled up; this helps to keep the coarse sand footing in place. The dirt underlying the sand is angled slightly to form a mild slope that aids in water runoff. The coarse sand footing can absorb all but the most torrential downpours.

A 32-foot string line was used to mark the perimeter. A stake was driven, the line attached, and used to scribe the outer edge. Stakes were set to mark post positions.

The first two posts are spaced 12 feet apart to mount a large swinging gate that will allow a tractor or truck inside to work the footing.

A 4-foot-wide gate should be installed next to the vehicle gate. Mark this gate post hole 4 feet and 8 inches (center to center) from one of the big gate post holes.

The remainder of the post holes are positioned at 7-foot intervals. Gate posts are 8-foot, pressure-treated 6 by 6-inch lumber. Treated, 7-foot, 4 by 4-inch posts are used for the rest of the structure.

Post holes for the regular posts were drilled 3 feet deep, and the gate post holes, 4 feet. It's best to put a foot of concrete in the bottom of the holes, especially in loose, sandy soil and if you plan to angle the walls of your round pen.

Although the Academy pen has straight walls, an outward angle of 5 to 10 degrees will avoid lots of knee bumps. Use sticks to brace the posts at the desired angle while the concrete sets, then backfill the holes with tamped dirt. Use your string line to check that each post is set at the correct distance from center. Remember that the gate posts will have to be set vertically for the gates to swing smoothly.

Once the concrete is set and the dirt is tamped around the posts, you can attach the fence planks. The bottom boards are up 1 foot from the ground, measured to the bottom of the board. The middle planks are centered on the posts, at 2½ feet from the ground. The top planks are 4 feet from the ground at the top of the plank. If the posts are too long, you'll

Here is a traditional round pen complete with a snubbing post in the center.

This modern round pen shuts out distractions, and the sides are sloped outward.

A large pen with smooth inside walls.

A small pen with solid walls that still allow for some air circulation. This one is complete with an observation deck.

Pipe is used to enclose this hot walker.

need to cut them off at this height. Cutting the posts at an angle will help keep them from rotting at the tops. Round the sharp edge of the post with a rasp to guard against injuries.

If the site is level, you can find the proper height for each plank by measuring from the bottom of the posts. If the site is not perfectly level, use a level to set each plank. You'll need to trim each board to fit, making sure that the planks break at the center of each post.

Put the planks on the insides of the posts. They can be attached with plain 16-penny nails, but I suggest ring-shank nails, wood screws, or long carriage bolts. In a small training corral, a loose nail can snag horse or rider. If you use bolts, you'll need to predrill the planks and posts, which can be time-consuming. The bolt heads will go on the inside of the pen, and must be flush with the wood to avoid injuries.

The gates can be wood or you can use prefabricated steel gate panels. The panels are lighter and less likely to sag. However, the wood gates can be built to match the rest of the pen.

To build the big vehicle gate, first measure the opening and make allowance for the hinges. Use 12-foot, 2 by 6-inch planks for the cross boards and 4-foot, 2 by 6-inch planks for the vertical boards. Lay out the cross boards spaced to match the walls of the pen, and nail them to the vertical boards. Add a third vertical board in the

middle to strengthen the gate. Flip the gate over and mate three more vertical boards to the first ones.

This gate is heavy, and most strap hinges won't support it. The best thing to use are pipe hinges to distribute the weight over a large area.

When the gate is hung, it's a good idea to install a gate rest. A cut-off section of 2 by 6 can be driven into the ground next to the gate post to support the gate. Once it's at just the right height, it can be nailed to the post. This will help keep the gate from sagging.

The walk-through gate is built like the bigger one, but without the center brace. Don't install a gate rest, either, because the horse might bang his leg on the rest.

Make sure your gates swing both in and out. And mount the inside of the gate flush with the inside surface of the pen wall so there is no protruding edge. The big gate posts are a good place to install a couple of tie rings, they should be at least horse eye-level high, but this is not possible on a 4-foot post.

Also make sure the walk-through gate can be easily latched and unlatched from both sides.

In a small training corral, a loose nail can snag horse or rider.

An attractive wood round pen with a solid gate, smooth walls that slope out, and a gap at the top to catch some breeze.

With the construction done, it's time to bring in the sand, if footing needs to be improved. To fill a 64-foot-diameter arena to a depth of 6 inches will require about 50 tons of sand. A light tractor can be used to spread the sand and level the surface. You don't want the sand so deep that the horse has to struggle in it. This can cause pulled ligaments and muscle strains. If the underlying dirt is hard, you can use a full 6 inches of sand. But if the underlying soil is spongy, loose, or sandy, you may only need to add 3 or 4 inches of sand. It's better to add a little sand at a time, rather than too much all at once.

For any round pen, it's handy to have a rack just outside the walk-through gate for training tools such as longe lines and whips.

Arenas

Because arenas are costly to build and maintain, it is practical for groups to build one for shared use. Riding clubs give the average horseman access to arena facilities that he perhaps can't afford privately.

Whether they are outdoors or covered, there are three basic shapes for arenas: rectangular with square corners, rectangular with rounded corners, and oval.

Rectangular arenas are commonly used for English training, particularly dressage. Western riding events generally call for oval arenas or rectangular arenas with rounded corners. However, horses can be schooled for almost all events in any arena, regardless of the arena shape.

Rodeo competitions can be held in any of the three types of arenas. However, bucking horses and roping cattle might hang up in corners. For this reason, a rectangular arena with rounded corners or an oval arena is preferable for these uses.

Buggy or carriage driving is best practiced in a large oval arena with banked corners.

Arena size depends on the activity. The American Quarter Horse Association recommends a minimum size of 100 by 200 feet for its shows. A spokesman for the AQHA competition program said that most western riding events—cutting, roping, reining, team penning, barrel racing, etc.—can be held in an arena of this size. However, he also said that competitors feel most comfortable in an arena that is 125 feet wide and 250 feet long. That size is also recommended by the National Cutting Horse Association for cutting horse competitions.

Many cutting horse trainers have square arenas that are 110 feet on a side. Another common sight on cutting horse outfits is a round pen up to 160 feet in diameter. The round pens are used to teach the young horses to follow and control cattle without relying on straight fence lines or corners to help. Team penning horses may also benefit from this kind of early training.

For a home arena, anything less than 100 feet wide and 150 feet long will feel cramped. This is true even if your objective is training pleasure horses. Because of the expense involved in an indoor arena, they may be smaller—75 wide by 120 long, for instance.

The Professional Rodeo Cowboys Association says there are no regulations on arena size for sanctioned rodeos, and that arena size may be as small as 180 by 300 feet, or even down to 135 by 240 feet and still be sufficient for bareback, saddle bronc, bull riding, calf roping, steer wrestling, and team roping.

There are also portable roping and riding arenas on the market, typically in 20-foot sections of pipe and wire mesh. Measurements range from 100 by 200 feet for roping, and 80 by 200 feet for general riding.

Most outdoor arenas feature post and rail fences of wood, welded pipe, or tubular steel panels. Other types of arena fence might be V-mesh on wood posts with a wood or pipe top rail. Some fences include heavy cable mounted through wood or metal posts.

If you plan to work cattle in the arena, it's best to stay with post and rail or pipe fences. Cattle quickly tear wire mesh fences apart. Although cable fences are nearly indestructible, I know of one roper who will tell you not to build one. He constructed a large roping arena using old telephone poles and heavy, twisted-steel cable. Although the cables were heavy and spaced only a foot apart, the roping cattle always tried to slip through. Often, new cattle would run right into the cable as if it weren't there.

The types of gates you choose will depend on how the arena is fenced. Solid steel panel gates hold up well and are suitable for walk-through or vehicle gates. Walk-through gates should be at least 4 feet wide. Vehicle gates should be at least 12 feet wide. Gates that can be opened from horseback are convenient and good practice for trail classes.

Longer gates need to be hung on extremely stout posts—either wood or pipe. Some long gates have a dolly wheel on the bottom to make them easier to handle.

The arena footing you choose should suit your type of riding. Most events require firm footing, with a thin, loose top layer. Speed events such as barrel racing and roping also favor this type of footing.

Deep ground will cause strains and sprains in your horses. Thoroughpins, sprained fetlocks, and pulled tendons will occur in horses worked in ground that has been disked too deep. At the other extreme, ground that is too hard can cause concussion injuries. For an arena that is heavily used, it is a good idea to work the ground regularly with a disk or harrow to keep the surface from becoming too compacted.

When picking a spot for an arena, look for a large, level area requiring minimum excavation. Ideally, the ground should slope slightly from the arena center to the sides to aid in drainage. A very gentle slope from one side to the other will accomplish the same thing. Once the surface has been graded, it should be expected to settle for 6 months to a year, or a roller can be used to hurry the process.

If you do the site work yourself, don't trust your eyes to determine if the surface is level. A transit is necessary to check the work.

Dirt is a common footing for arenas, but is easily affected by weather. It's dusty when dry and can turn into a bog when it's too wet.

Native soils can be improved by adding processed wood fibers such as sawdust, wood chips, or bark. However, these materials tend to freeze rapidly and thaw slowly, and require good drainage. In cold climates, these materials are better suited to indoor arena footing.

Coarse sand works well for arena footing, provided it is not too deep. Sand also works well when added to improve the resiliency and drainage of native soils. The combination will be lighter and easier to work up. Pure sand must be applied over a firm base to stay in place.

There are commercial products available to improve arena footing. A common product is a compound of shredded or beaded rubber. Mixed with dirt, shredded rubber provides excellent footing and good drainage. However, a horse who eats rubber can colic, so if you use this material for arena footing, don't use the arena as a

The arena footing you choose should suit your type of riding.

104

turnout pen. These commercial products
are also quite expensive.

Controlling dust is a problem with most
arenas, particularly indoor arenas. In most
facilities, some type of watering system is
used to control arena dust. Some professional arenas feature a sprinkler system
mounted on the arena fence. Others rely
on water trucks to keep the dust down.

The best approach is to look for footing
materials that cause a minimum of dust.
Although this may be costlier initially, it
will reduce maintenance and protect the
health of horses and riders.

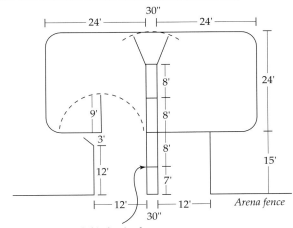

*Drop-gate behind animal,
other partitions may be slide-gates.*

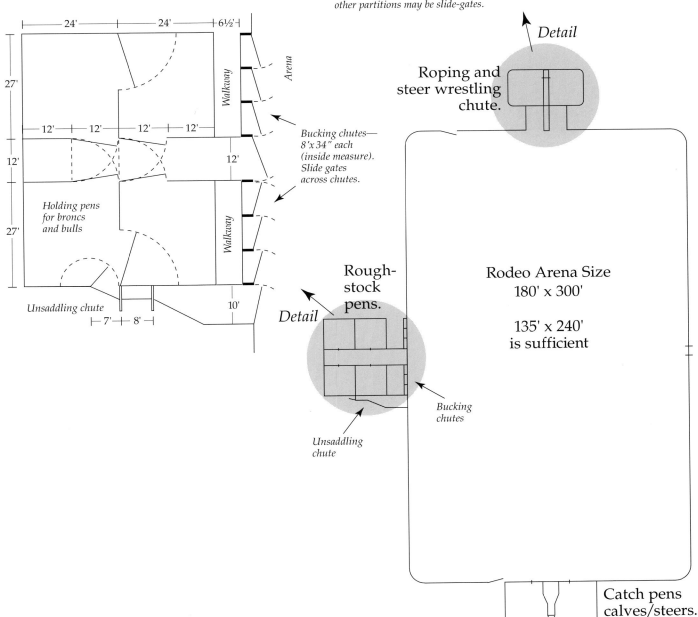

*Holding pens
for broncs
and bulls*

Unsaddling chute

*Bucking chutes—
8' x 34" each
(inside measure).
Slide gates
across chutes.*

Roping and
steer wrestling
chute.

Detail

Rough-
stock
pens.

Detail

*Unsaddling
chute*

*Bucking
chutes*

Rodeo Arena Size
180' x 300'

135' x 240'
is sufficient

Catch pens
calves/steers.

FENCE MATERIALS

13

Good fencing is the best insurance for your horses.

THE FIRST step in building fence is to check with your county or regional building department for any fence requirements. Call the utility company to locate any underground wire. If you live in a development governed by covenants, check on those, too.

If you're not certain about boundary lines, a survey might be in order. Having to move a fence line a few feet because of a border dispute with your neighbor can add considerably to the labor cost of the finished fence.

Once your fence lines are established, you might want to use grid paper to make a scaled map of your fence plan. This will help in ordering materials and in determining placement of gates, walk-throughs, water tanks, and feeders. You can also use the scale map to estimate actual costs of various materials.

In tight pasture situations, some horsemen prefer not to have any squared corners, so they round everything off. This helps a timid horse avoid being trapped in a corner. Any corner angles of less than 90 degrees should be avoided.

Posts

Although the type of posts you choose will depend on the type of fence you build, there are some general rules.

Posts should be stout and strong enough to withstand the impact of a running horse. The collision might injure the horse; but if the post breaks, the horse can be impaled, which almost guarantees serious or fatal injury.

About one-third of a post should be buried. This is true of wood, steel pipe, vinyl, or T-posts. Brace posts, gate posts, and corner posts are strongest when set in concrete. However, it is better to pour a concrete collar around the bottom of a post and fill the rest of the hole with dirt than to fill the hole to the top with concrete. If there's no give in the post, it's more likely to break or bend above the ground.

Buried wood posts will last longer if they are pressure-treated with a wood preservative. Treated posts cost more initially, but are the best long-term investment. Treated posts can last up to four times as long as untreated. Steel posts

Today, we have lots more fence material choices than our forefathers, who used whatever was at hand.

106

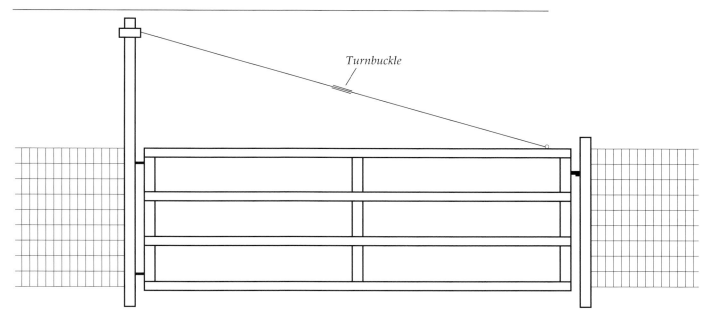

Swing gate.

will last longer if they are coated with a rust-preventing paint.

Railroad ties, when available, make excellent fence posts because they are treated with creosote and will last for decades. Furthermore, they are stout and wide, with plenty of surface to nail to.

Gates

Consider whether you will need to access the pasture or corral with a pickup or tractor. If so, a gate width of at least 10 feet will be necessary, and 12 feet would be better. Standard width for a walk-through gate is 4 feet.

When positioning gates, consider access to driveways, feed storage areas, stables or barns, and riding areas. The use will help determine what type of gate to install. In snowy climates, you will want to position gates in places where there are usually no snowdrifts, and to use gate designs that won't be hampered by snow.

Horses tend to congregate around fence gates, particularly at feeding time. Good gates require extra-heavy gate posts and strong hinges. Latches should also be strong, easy for a person to use, but hard for a horse to open. Some examples of good latches are shown on these pages.

To reduce strain on gate hinges, it's helpful to have a gate rest to support the

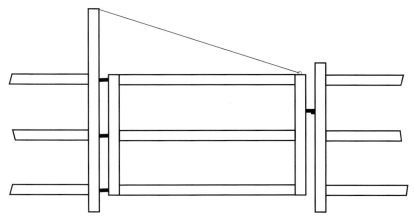

Walk-through gate.

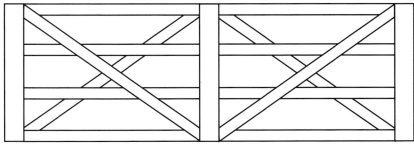

Wood pasture gate.

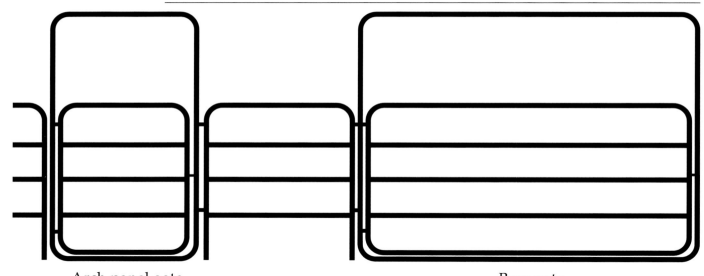

Arch panel gate.   Bow gate.

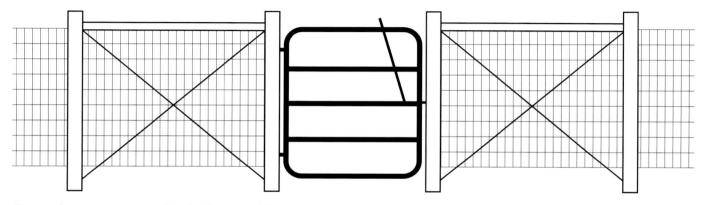

Braced gate posts and tubular steel horseman's gate.

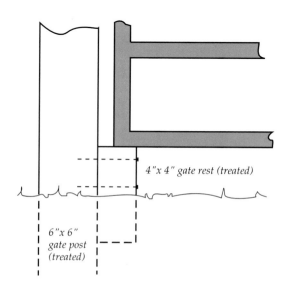

4"x 4" gate rest (treated)

6"x 6"
gate post
(treated)

gate when it is closed, and another for the full-open position. This saves a lot of wear and tear on the hinges, because they are stressed only when the gate is moved.

Gates that swing away from the horses are safest. But ideally, a swinging gate should go both ways.

Tubular steel panels make excellent gates. They are strong and relatively light. A sturdy wood gate can be very heavy, and must be properly engineered to hold up. In large pastures, wire gates are common, and they are the most cost-effective type of gate.

Aluminum gates are common but dangerous. The thin aluminum sheet metal used in these gates can have sharp edges. And the material is comparatively flimsy, which can lead to break-down from metal fatigue caused by wind or pushy horses.

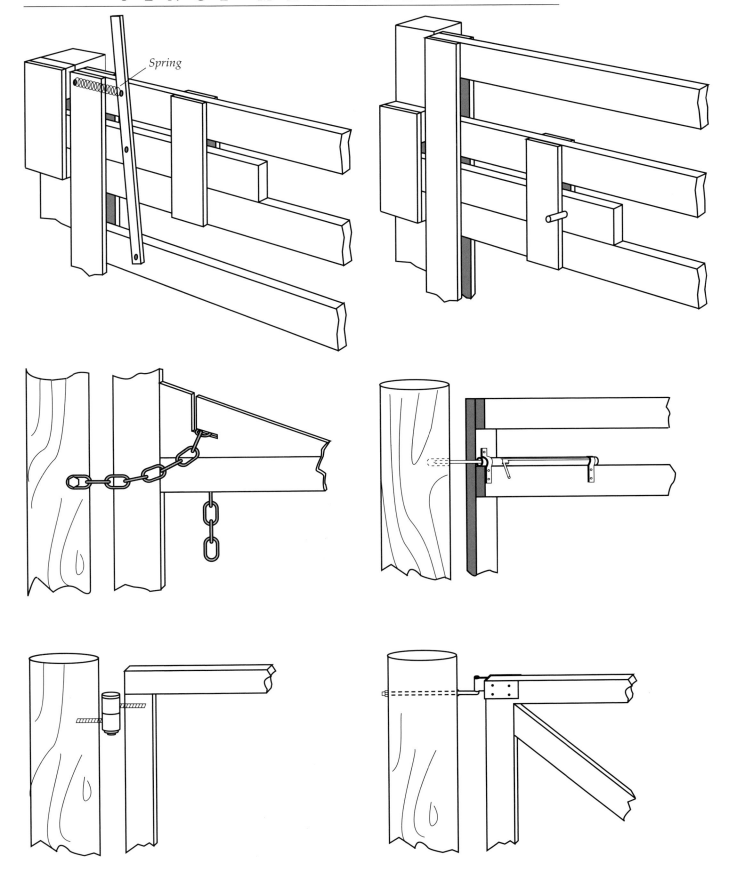

Spring

Although pipe panels can be locked together, this panel is going to be secured to a wood post for greater stability. Post holes can be dug by hand, or by tractor-mounted augers.

On the left side of the post is a common gate hanger bolt that is threaded into a partially predrilled hole.

What Kind of Fence?

Because pens, corrals, and pastures each serve a different purpose, you may consider several types of fencing materials. Some planning consultants say that you should choose just one type of fence for all your needs, because this will make your property look more attractive. But that advice makes absolutely no horse sense.

A fence is a tool, and the most important consideration should be choosing the right tool for the job. Some of the most attractive and professional horse outfits use many types of fencing.

No matter the size of the enclosure, a horse fence should be a minimum of 4 feet high. For large horses and stallions, higher fences are necessary. As a rule, the higher the fence, the safer the fence. When a horse can stick his head over, under, or through a fence, it is more dangerous than if he can only see through that fence.

Another basic rule: The smaller the enclosure, the stronger and safer it must be. A horse has a better chance of running into a single protruding nail in a small pen than he does in a 40-acre pasture. And when you put a horse in a small enclosure, he's more likely to want out than if he's in a large and roomy area. This is especially true for young, untrained horses not accustomed to confinement.

110

RAMBLIN ROSE RANCH

Entrance gates can present a tremendous first impression.

There is no one best fencing material for every application. The layout of your property, the type and personalities of your horses, geography, climate, and the size of your bank account all play roles in influencing the best fence for you.

Even veteran horsemen may be surprised at the wide variety of fence materials. In the past few decades, there have been tremendous advances in designing safer, more attractive, and longer-lasting fence materials for horses. Whether you've been around horses all your life or you're new to horse ownership, the information here should help you make knowledgeable choices about which material will suit your circumstances.

Horse outfits require strong, long-lasting fences that minimize hazards to the animals. Fences must also keep out intruders. In a tradition dating back to the early days of ranching, rural areas in many western states are still regarded as open range. Under the laws in those areas, it is the property owner's responsibility to fence out his neighbors' livestock, and the livestock owner is not generally responsible for property damage caused by his wandering animals. This policy usually does not apply to state and federal highways.

In suburban areas the problem is not wandering sheep and cattle, but roving children and pets. Children are strongly attracted to horses, and dogs like to chase horses. Because property owners may be held legally responsible for any injuries that take place on their land—even to "guests" who were not invited—fences in residential areas must serve double duty. They must keep horses in and unwanted trespassers out.

The fencing materials that work well for horses generally fall into four categories: wood (plank, pole, and split-rail), smooth wire, electric, and synthetics. All have advantages and disadvantages. Many people combine materials and avoid some of the disadvantages.

Wood

Wood plank or board fences, especially white ones, are beautiful additions to any horse property, and are one of the safest for horses. Plank fences work well for pasture fencing and corrals, although they may be less than ideal for small pens and exercise runs where wood chewing may be a problem.

A drawback of wood fences is that they are costly and require a great deal of up-

Split-rail fences are extremely attractive, but are expensive and usually short-lived.

Split rails must be notched into the post.

keep. Many people build plank fences at the most visible entrance to their property, and use less expensive wire fencing elsewhere. Plank fencing also works well for enclosing small pastures (paddocks) of less than 5 acres, where aesthetic considerations can be balanced with a relatively small outlay for necessary materials. Plank fencing is frequently used for outdoor arenas.

If you select wood fencing, use thick boards and stout posts. Boards should be a minimum of 2 inches thick and 6 inches wide. One-inch boards are more easily broken and can impale or badly gash a horse. Posts should be at least 6 inches in diameter and 7 to 8 feet long. If possible, use a hardwood such as oak, cypress, or juniper, although a softwood such as pine is satisfactory if treated. There are commercial anti-chewing treatments that can be applied to wood to discourage chewing, although some horses will go right on with the habit. Other options are cribbing straps, metal strips on the edge of boards, and an electric wire in the right place.

Treated posts and lumber used as pasture fencing.

Many people build plank fences at the most visible entrance to their property, and use less expensive wire fencing elsewhere.

Planks should be on the horse side of the fence. Note that the gate rests against the post so it can't be pushed out.

The flat plank on the top reinforces the fence and protects the tops of the posts from moisture.

White paint gives the traditional board-fence look.

For mares and geldings, a fence height of 48 inches is the minimum, and taller is safer. For stallion pastures and turnout pens, fencing should ideally be 7 feet high. Obviously, a wood fence this high would be expensive, which is why some stallion owners prefer to use pipe, chain-link, or some variety of wire-mesh fencing.

A 7-foot fence might at first seem excessive, but a stallion on the loose must be considered a dangerous animal, and should be handled accordingly. There are many possible consequences of a stallion escaping, and all of them pose legal liabilities.

A well-mannered and trustworthy stallion might be securely confined by a fence 5 feet high. Even so, you might run a hot wire along the top of the fence, or on the inside about chest-high.

Wooden pole constructions, such as the sawbuck style often seen in mountain pastures, make strong and attractive fences, but can be costly, particularly in non-timbered areas. However, in rough, rocky terrain where digging post holes is nearly impossible, the sawbuck fence may be the best option. Some owners cut their own poles. However, if the poles are not treated with a preservative, they will rot much quicker than pretreated lumber. If you do cut your own poles, it's advisable to strip the bark, which might contain insects and moisture.

Of the types of wood fencing, split-rail fences are the most expensive. They are strong, fairly easy to build, and have a pleasant appearance. Most are made of cedar or redwood, which have great resistance to rot. One major disadvantage, however, is the way the rails fit into the posts. After several years, the rails loosen and can drop out.

Rather than using split rails, you might consider post and pole fences. The poles feature tapered ends that fit into drilled holes in the posts. The heartwood of the poles is very strong, and shrinkage is minimal.

Many horsemen find it economical to combine pole construction with smooth wire or wire mesh fencing. This kind of fence is not as attractive as an all-wood fence, but it is less costly.

Wire

Wire fences are popular on all sizes of horse operations, and for good reasons. They are relatively inexpensive to build, and can be attractive when they are correctly constructed. Fences can utilize double-twisted smooth wire or wire mesh. Cable is sometimes used for paddocks, runs, or small pens, but seldom for longer stretches such as around pastures.

The major disadvantage of wire fences is that horses might not respect them. This is particularly a problem in cross fencing between pastures, a situation where horses will socialize and sometimes fight over the fence. Horses will also push, pull, and reach through a fence to get at grass on the other side, especially if their diets are inadequate. Good nutrition, along with mowing the grass along the outside of the fence, can help prevent this problem.

Double-twisted smooth wire is the most economical fencing material, but it is very susceptible to stretching and sagging. Proper construction and maintenance are essential for this kind of fence.

Barbed wire is absolutely not recommended for horse fencing, and the smaller the enclosure, the more dangerous it is. In small pastures, sooner or later, horses will run into or be shoved into a fence.

A mesh wire fence should be high enough so a horse cannot reach over it to graze on the other side. That will result in the fence being mashed down. Some horsemen string one or two strands of smooth wire above the mesh wire to prevent the problem. A 2 by 6-inch top board will serve the same purpose. It looks better than a strand of wire, but requires more labor to install, costs more, and will need painting or treatment with a wood preservative.

Staples driven snug to the post, but not far enough in to crimp the wire.

Here's a superstout combination of railroad ties, planks, and V-mesh wire.

Another board and V-mesh combination. Notice the posts have been cut at an angle to drain off the water.

In enclosures for broodmares with foals, horizontal boards midway up the fence on the inside can prevent the foals from crashing into the fence as they run alongside their mothers. These boards also make the fences more visible, which helps to prevent accidents.

Wire fences can utilize wood posts or steel T-posts or a combination of both. Wood post construction takes more work, but looks better. Furthermore, it is better suited to enclosing small pastures, because metal posts can be bent by a horse scratching on them. Horses also sometimes impale themselves on T-posts. The danger is less in large pastures than in smaller enclosures. Safety caps and electric wires are two methods to make these posts safer.

On the positive side, steel posts help to ground a fence in an electric storm, although they are no substitute for actual lightning rods. And, steel posts are less expensive than wood, and they last for many years.

Wire-mesh fence comes in many designs, widths, and strengths. The most common design used for horses is a non-

V-mesh with one strand of smooth wire to keep horses from leaning over the mesh.

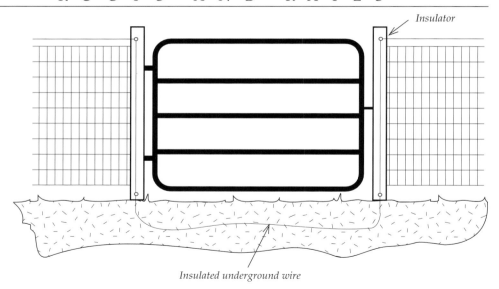

Insulator

Insulated underground wire

climb, 2 by 4-inch rectangular mesh, or variations such as V-mesh, also called diamond mesh. Although V-mesh is very safe for horses, it is costly and fairly rigid, and could be hard for the amateur builder to work with. If you haven't had a lot of experience, it's probably best to stick with the standard rectangular mesh designs, or to hire a professional to install V-mesh.

In either case, a tight weave with no openings more than 2 inches wide is best. Larger openings in mesh fence may allow a horse to catch a hoof, which can lead to injuries. Furthermore, a horse is less likely to catch a shoe, causing hoof damage, in a tightly woven fence. The open-weave patterns are sometimes referred to as hog fence or sheep fence, and are best left to confining those species of livestock.

Wire mesh fence is either spot-welded or woven with interlocking joints. The jointed wire works best on contours, because the fence can flex and accommodate dips and rises in the ground. Additionally, it can better withstand the impact of a horse hitting it without breaking, a problem with welded wire. The spot-welded fence doesn't have much give, but costs less. It works well for slightly sloping pastures.

Cyclone, or chain-link, works well for pens, runs, stallion enclosures, and may be desirable for pasture or paddock fencing in high-density population areas. However, it is prohibitively expensive and has the disadvantage of not being malleable enough to be straightened once it is damaged. Also, sharp wire ends on the top and bottom of chain link fence can lacerate a horse's head or neck, or punch a hole in a leg. When using chain-link fence, it is recommended that a pipe be run along the top of the fence and a tension wire along the bottom to prevent injury and to strengthen the fence. This fence should be at least 5 feet high and should be supported on steel posts that are at least 1⅞ inches in diameter. For a stallion enclosure, a height of 7 feet is recommended. Generally, cyclone fence should be installed by a professional fence company.

Electric

Many horsemen use electric fencing on at least part of their enclosures. This fencing is generally inexpensive, and good to fence-train young horses. On the down side, electric fence is often difficult to see, and horses may run right through it. It is also easily damaged by large wildlife, and it stretches easily. A fallen branch, tall weeds, or contact with a metal post or gate can short-circuit a system, rendering the whole thing ineffective. Low-voltage

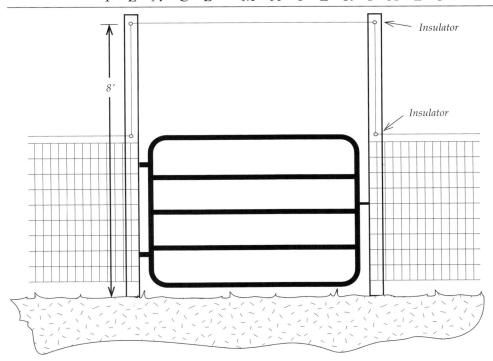

fence chargers are best to avoid injuries to horses. Electric fences are not recommended for areas where children might wander into contact.

Electric fences can be built in much less time than is required for other kinds of fences. And they are relatively easy to take down and move to other locations. If you rent pasture, this can be a great advantage.

The best uses for electrified systems are as temporary fencing and as a complement to wood or wire fences. Using an electric hot wire along the top of a smooth-wire fence, or to prevent chewing of a pole or plank fence will save on repairs and replacements.

Some all-electric fences use three to four strands of 12-gauge smooth wire on posts spaced 12 to 15 feet apart. It's a good idea to add something to increase visibility, too. Some new types of fencing feature aluminum filaments woven into a plastic ribbon-like fabric. The fabric is tightened with clips that are attached to the fence posts.

Some people recommend placing the electric fence insulators on the outside of the fence posts, so that the insulators won't get snagged and broken. Others suggest placing insulators on the inside to prevent chewing damage to posts. Some

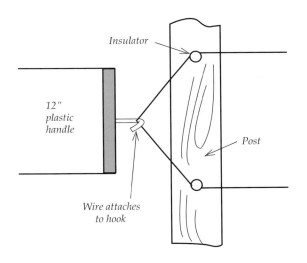

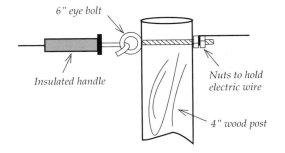

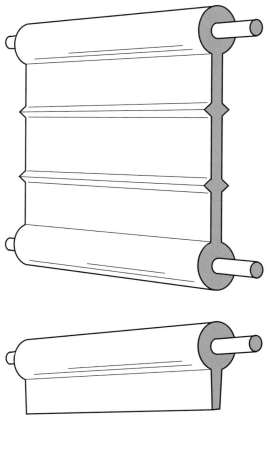

Polymer and wire combinations are, from top: two-wire strip, one-wire strip, and plastic-coated wire. These are more visible, stronger, and safer than wire alone.

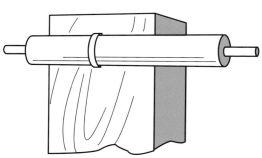

trained, you can save a few pennies by leaving the fence turned off part of the time. Most horses will get in the habit of leaving the fence alone.

All fence chargers should carry an intermittent current, and should be certified by the Underwriters Laboratory. Insulated handles can be purchased to bridge fence gates and allow the horseman to lead his horses in and out of the pasture without getting jolted. Other ways of handling gates are illustrated in this chapter.

Synthetics

Synthetics offer a host of advantages for fencing. Their uniformity makes them easy to build with, they don't require painting, horses seldom chew on their slick surfaces, they don't rot or rust, and won't splinter. Despite the higher initial cost, most makers of synthetic fence assure their customers that the long-term savings in maintenance will repay the cost difference.

There are many styles of synthetic fencing, most of them resembling the more traditional wood and wire fencing. Some actually incorporate wood, wire, or steel in their design.

A popular substitute for the traditional white plank or pole fencing is a rigid PVC or vinyl fence. Vinyl fence can be bought in sections or built to order. Some companies offer an assortment of colors. Vinyl fences are held together with bolts or screws, as well as glued couplings. Some simply snap together. Sometimes PVC boards are used in combination with traditional wood posts. But synthetic post fences are also available.

One problem with rigid PVC fences is that they have a wide range of thermal expansion and contraction. Heat can cause these fences to sag or bow. In extreme cold weather, low-quality synthetics might shatter on impact. The highest quality vinyl fences feature internal ribs and are thick-walled, and their assembly allows for expansion and contraction. Ultraviolet inhibitors are used in the top-quality vinyl products.

Many PVC board fences are designed to come apart on impact. This prevents the boards from breaking, and keeps the horse from getting hurt. Unfortunately, this factor also allows the horse to escape. This type of fence, therefore, is not suitable for stallion enclosures.

designs allow you to run the wires through the posts. Since most horses learn quickly to respect hot wires, it's probably best to put the insulators inside. This keeps horses from leaning or scratching on posts, and the posts are protected against wood chewing. To confine most horses, only the top and bottom wires need to be charged. Once the horses are fence-

Synthetic fence combines the look of plank fence with the advantages of no maintenance.

Another type of synthetic fencing is polymer strips with wire or cable running through them on the top and bottom edges. This solves the visibility problem of smooth wire fences but not the sagging problem. And horses may push against these wider surfaces more than they would push on wire. So a design that allows for tightening is best.

Application of synthetics to fencing is often seen around construction sites, where synthetic mesh is common. Several weights, heights, and designs are offered for livestock fencing.

Another synthetic fence variation is a hybrid of the standard wood plank fence. Wood boards are permanently sheathed in polyethylene. The sheath protects the wood from rot, splintering, and insects. According to one manufacturer, the product costs about the same as a quality wood fence finished with a primer and two coats of paint. But the synthetic-sheathed boards and posts never require new paint. These fences are constructed just like regular wood fences, but special caps are fitted over the board and post ends to create a watertight seal.

Many synthetic fences are guaranteed by their manufacturers. If you invest in this kind of fence, be sure to get a guarantee in writing. Also, try to deal with a reputable

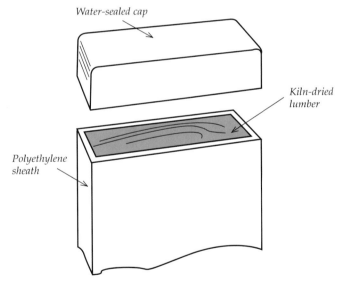

Water-sealed cap

Kiln-dried lumber

Polyethylene sheath

manufacturer or dealer. When synthetic fencing first appeared, some of it failed to live up to the manufacturers' promises. Some dealers and some makers went out of business after only a few years, making lifetime guarantees worthless. Since then, however, many of the problems with synthetic materials have been overcome.

BUILDING FENCE

Careful planning is the most important stage of this process.

Building Wire Fence

It's helpful to mow the area along the planned fence line if it's overgrown with grass and weeds. This will make the job easier, and maybe safer if you live in snake country. If a tractor isn't available, use a power mower or hand tools.

Consider that twisted wire or mesh wire fencing is not well suited to curves. One solution is to use wire for the straight sections, and to handle any necessary curves with posts and boards.

In western cattle country, where wire fences might enclose thousands of acres, fence posts can be spaced up to 16 feet apart. However, for the property owner with anything less than 100 acres to fence, post spacing will be between 8 and 12 feet. For hills and depressions, it is advisable to narrow the space between posts. Spacing is up to you, but remember that it's easier to put in an extra post at first than it is to add one after the wire is up and stretched.

Going back to your grid-paper layout plan, plot the number of posts you'll need. Add more for corner-post braces and cross braces, which we'll discuss later.

Generally, line posts, whose primary function is to support the fence wire, can be round (minimum 3-inch diameter) posts, 4 by 4-inch square posts, or steel T-posts.

In most parts of the country, and for most types of soil, 18 inches is deep enough for line post holes. Therefore, a 52-inch-high fence, using 47-inch wire mesh with a strand of twisted wire on top, will require 6-foot posts. In rocky or loose soil, use longer posts and sink them deeper. A good

rule of thumb is that a third of the post should be underground.

Corner and brace posts, which anchor the wire, are the keystones of a wire fence. If they fail, an entire section of fence will fail with them. The standard length for corner posts is 8 feet, and the standard diameter is 8 inches. Brace posts should also be 8 feet long and at least 8 inches in diameter, measured at the small end. Even larger posts may be required for hanging heavy gates.

Some property owners may be tempted to use substandard materials in building pasture fences. But horses put more stress on a small pasture than they would on a larger one, so your smaller pastures need to meet minimum building standards.

If you are fencing a large pasture, renting a tractor equipped with a power auger can be a big labor saver. A power auger can dig 20 holes in the time it takes a man to dig just 1, and can repay your rental costs in labor savings. There are also power drivers for rent that will speed up the job of tamping. Still another option is a two-man power auger, which you can usually rent from a farm supply store or equipment rental operation.

Steel posts are set with a steel post driver, which is a heavy hollow tube with two handles. These can be rented or perhaps borrowed from a neighbor.

No matter how you dig the holes and set the posts, the fence line should be as straight as possible. For small pastures, you can stake out your end points and run a string or wire between them, spacing the post holes or T-post sites under the wire.

For large pastures, begin with two

sighting stakes along the fence line. With the help of an assistant, place marker stakes to hold a string or wire.

An easy way to mark post holes is take two thin posts and tie them together with a string as long as the spacing you want between your posts. The device is similar to the one used by football officials to measure yardage. Begin at a corner, and mark each post site with a small stake, leapfrogging one post past the other.

The corner posts and brace posts are set first. An 8-foot corner post and the brace posts should be set about 3 feet deep. The wood line posts will need holes about 18 inches deep. If the soil is sandy, it may be a good idea to set corner and brace posts in concrete. Make sure that the wide end of the post goes in the ground. And be sure that any splits and cracks are turned away from where the wire will be stapled to the post.

When filling dirt in around a post, don't push in any rocks. They won't tamp in well, and if you ever have to dig the post up to replace it, the rocks will make the job harder. A long tamping bar will make it easier to tamp the dirt properly. Add a little dirt at a time, tamping it well before adding more dirt. Use a carpenter's level to make sure your posts are absolutely vertical.

With your corner and brace posts set, add the horizontal bracing posts. Use a chain saw or a chisel to notch the vertical posts about ½-inch deep at the height you'll install the horizontal posts. Carefully measure the distance from notch to notch, and if necessary, cut your horizontal post to match the dimension. Use ¼-inch or ⅜-inch steel dowel pins, spikes, or rebar to hold the horizontal posts securely in place. Wrap the ends of each horizontal post with steel wire to prevent splitting.

Double-wrap four strands of 9-gauge galvanized steel wire, or use double-twisted smooth wire diagonally across the front of each brace. Staple the wires in place with long, galvanized fence staples to prevent them from slipping down on the posts. Use a piece of scrap wood as a lever to tighten the diagonal wire, and leave the lever in place so that you can tighten the brace in the future.

This basic brace structure is the same for corners and braces, and for gate posts. For a straight fence line, braces should be spaced about every 300 feet, and as close as 165 feet on curved fence sections. Part of the reason for these spacings is that

Acreage Guide

160 acres requires 2 miles or 640 rods of fence to enclose

80 acres requires 1½ miles or 480 rods of fence to enclose

40 acres requires 1 mile or 320 rods of fence to enclose

20 acres requires 240 rods of fence to enclose

10 acres requires 160 rods to enclose

5 acres 120 rods

20 sq. rods

¼ mile = 1,320 ft. or 80 rods
½ mile = 2,640 ft. or 160 rods
1 mile = 5,280 ft. or 320 rods

1 rod = 16½ ft.
10 rods = 165 ft.
20 rods = 330 ft.

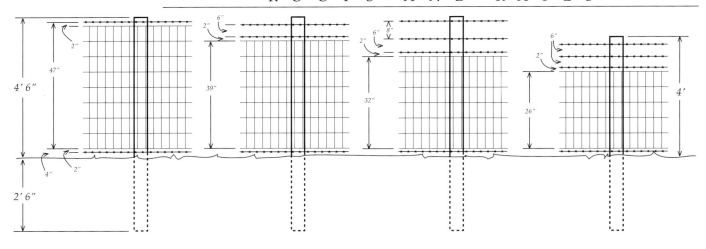

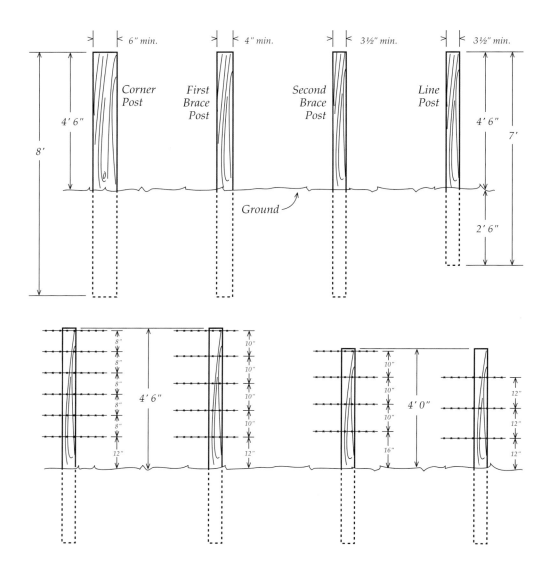

A power auger is a good idea if you have many postholes to dig.

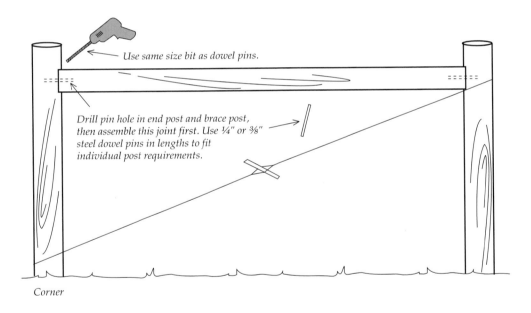

Use same size bit as dowel pins.

Drill pin hole in end post and brace post, then assemble this joint first. Use ¼" or ⅜" steel dowel pins in lengths to fit individual post requirements.

Corner

When all your posts are firmly set, it's time to string wire.

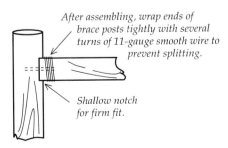

After assembling, wrap ends of brace posts tightly with several turns of 11-gauge smooth wire to prevent splitting.

Shallow notch for firm fit.

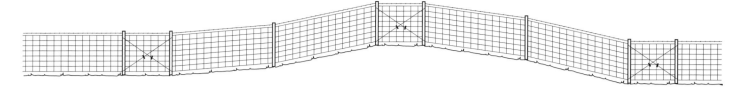

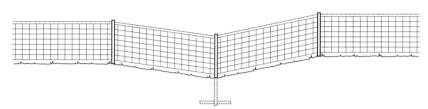

most woven wire is sold in 10- or 20-rod rolls. A rod equals 16½ feet, so a little multiplication shows you where to space your braces to avoid wasting wire. You may need more braces, however, if the land is uneven or your fences must span creek beds or ditches.

Once you've completed the corners and braces, set the line posts. The fence will look better if the tops of the posts are all the same height, so make a mark on your post-hole digger and use it to keep all your holes the same depth. When all your posts are firmly set, it's time to string wire.

Woven wire or twisted wire must be stretched, like a spring, to work properly. Tensioning the wire helps it retain its shape as it expands and contracts with changes in temperature. Corner and line posts resist the pull of the fence, while line posts primarily hold the wire taut and in position.

When possible, install the wire on the inside of the fence to prevent horses from loosening the staples when they push on the wire. Use 1½-inch staples to attach the wire to the posts, because smaller staples tend to work loose. Staples will hold

better if you angle them slightly across the grain of the wood. And don't hammer them in so deep that they mash the wire against the post—this leads to broken wire and shorter fence life.

Installing Mesh Wire

Begin by positioning the roll upright about 16 feet from a corner post. Unroll enough fence fabric to reach beyond the post and then remove enough of the vertical stay wires so that you can wrap the wire ends around the post with another 6 inches to spare.

Beginning with the center wire, wrap it tight around the post and then twist it back on itself with five or six tight wraps. Attach the wire to the post with staples.

Continue this process with each of the horizontal wires, watching the tension on each to keep the first vertical stay wire parallel to the post.

Once the horizontal wires are all attached, unroll the fence fabric alongside the fence posts, keeping the bottom wire close to the bottoms of the posts. Prop the wire up against the posts with extra posts, or use baling wire to tie it temporarily in place.

Stretching the woven wire correctly requires a fence puller that will apply an even force across the end of the fabric. Special fence pullers and clamps can be rented and are recommended. You can, however, improvise your own fence puller.

Understretching or overstretching the fence can cause problems. Overstretching will take all the spring out of your fence so that it won't be adaptable to thermal changes. Wire expands in heat and contracts in cold. If you use a tractor to stretch your fence, make sure you don't pull it too tight.

During the stretching process, check along the entire fence line to be sure that the wire isn't snagged on anything. The stay wires should remain vertical. If they don't, you have too much pull on the top or bottom of the fabric. If your fence has tension curves on the line wires, the fence is properly stretched when the tension curves are about half flattened out and the fence is springy along its entire length.

Before cutting the length you need from the roll, attach the fence to the line posts on the high points, then in the depressions. If you should need to slacken the tension or tighten the fence fabric to accommodate these irregularities, and especially if you need to pull additional wire from the roll, you'll be thankful you didn't cut away from the roll earlier.

When the entire fence is correctly adjusted, you can fasten the line wires one at a time, beginning at the top. Three staples —top, middle, and bottom—should be enough for each post. Clips are used to attach wire mesh to steel T-posts.

Once you've attached all your line wires, you can cut the fence fabric and attach the horizontal wires to your end post, using the same technique you employed to fasten the wire to the first corner post. Give yourself a little extra line wire, as it's a lot easier to cut off some extra wire than to try to splice extra wire to the ends if you come up short.

The last step is to run a twisted smooth wire or a board along the top of the fence. Stretch this wire with a regular fence stretcher, then drive a staple into each line post.

Installing Smooth Wire

Smooth wire fences vary from three to seven strands, with five strands being standard. The higher the fence, the less likely that a horse will reach over it to nibble vegetation on the other side. Double-twisted smooth wire is stronger than a single strand. Use heavy wire such as 12.5 gauge; it will save on repair and will last longer.

Once your posts are in place, wrap the top wire around the corner post and tie it off with five or six wraps around itself. Anchor it with 1½-inch galvanized staples, angled slightly, but don't mash the wire.

Unroll the wire to the next corner or brace post. Attach a fence clamp, or twist a loop in the end of the wire, then use a stretcher to tighten the wire enough that it does not sag. Staple or clip the wire to each post. Then, cut the end free from the roll and wrap it around the end post to start stringing another strand.

Work from top to bottom, making sure that each strand is evenly spaced on the posts. You may want to add vertical stay wires to strengthen the fence and prevent sagging. The stay wires have a forked end that allows you to twist them down over your horizontal strands.

Wire Fence Guidelines

When cross-fencing a pasture, you can strengthen your fence by cleating a 2 by 4-inch stud to the side of the post that is stapled. Use 16-penny nails to attach the stud to the post. A costlier alternative is to run strands or wire mesh on both sides of the posts.

Each year, some pastured animals are killed by lightning traveling down a wire fence. If you live in an area of frequent lightning storms, you should ground your

A curved fence should be only half to two-thirds as tight as a straight fence section.

127

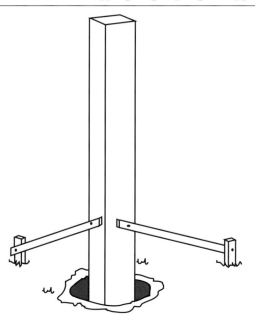

Do not stretch fence fabric or wire around a corner that changes the direction of the fence more than 45 degrees. Tie the fence off on a braced post at the apex of the turn, and start with a fresh section from that point.

Building Board Fence

Although a plank fence doesn't present nearly the technical difficulties of a wire fence, some attention to detail will improve its strength, appearance, and longevity.

Posts should be spaced 8 feet apart, measured from center to center, to accommodate standard lumber sizes. The best posts for fencing are those that are naturally resistant to rot and insects, such as redwood and cedar. However, these are expensive. Railroad ties or pressure-treated lumber, either hardwood or pine, can be used instead.

Minimum standard sizes for posts are 6 inches in diameter and 7 feet long. Round poles should be at least 6 inches in diameter. Boards should be 2 inches thick and at least 6 inches wide. Here again, a grid map will help you order lumber and supplies.

Digging holes and setting posts are generally the same as in wire fence construction, although brace posts and braced corner posts are not required. It is, however, advisable to set corner and gate posts in concrete.

Begin with the corner posts. Dig the holes a little deeper than a third the length of your posts. Backfill each hole just enough to bring the post up to the desired height. Gravel can be used in the bottom of the hole for this purpose; it's less likely to settle than dirt.

When all your corner posts are set and plumbed, drive a nail in the top of the posts and another nail a foot from the bottom. Then stretch string lines between the corner posts and use them to plumb and position each of the line posts. If you plan

wire fence. A galvanized steel rod, 10 to 12 feet long, should be driven into the ground far enough to reach permanent moisture. Use 11-gauge wire to connect fence lines to the rod. It's recommended to ground the fence every 50 rods, which is 825 feet. It's also advisable to ground the fence in corners where horses tend to congregate.

If your fence includes curves, be sure to run the wire on the outside of the posts on the curves so that the posts hold the tension. A curved fence should be only half to two-thirds as tight as a straight fence section. The sharper the curve, the less tension needed.

to set the posts in concrete, brace each post first. Then you can work quickly with the concrete without worrying about positioning the posts.

For anchoring posts, the concrete mix should be thin: one part cement, three parts sand, and five parts gravel. Use enough water so that the concrete mixture slumps off the shovel easily. Shovel the mixture into the post hole, then use a trowel to smooth the top of the concrete into a slightly conical shape. This will divert water from the post and help prevent rotting.

Allow the posts to set for at least 24 hours before removing the braces or attaching the cross boards. If the concrete pulls away from the posts, fill the cavities with roofing cement to prevent water from seeping into the posts.

When attaching horizontal boards, nail them to the inside of the posts so that horses can't loosen the nails by pushing on the boards. You can use either 8-, 10-, 12-, or 16-foot planks. You can use galvanized nails, or better still, predrill the boards and use wood screws. Drive the nails 1½ to 2 inches back from the ends of the planks to prevent splitting or cracking.

It's a good idea to use a cordless drill to predrill the nail holes, using a bit half the diameter of the nail. This guides the nail in straight and prevents splitting the board.

If you use 16-foot boards, you can make your fence stronger by staggering the boards so that the first top board is 16 feet, the second board is 8 feet, the third is 16, and so on. This adds rigidity to the fence and spreads stress out to keep one post from being pushed out of alignment.

Before attaching boards, check them for bows and crowns. Bows are boards that are bent along the widest edge, and crowns are bends along the narrow edge.

Install a crown facing up; this will help prevent sagging.

Don't butt the ends of the planks tight. Leave about a ¼-inch gap to allow for swelling, heat expansion, and contraction. Also, if you have to cut the end off a treated board, be sure to paint preservative over the raw end.

Unless you used unfinished lumber, you'll probably want to paint your fence. Paint the boards and posts with a primer coat, then apply two top coats. A good-quality exterior latex paint should hold up well. Although white paint has traditionally been the color of choice, many horsemen are turning to black paint. Lower maintenance is the reason—black paint doesn't need to be scraped or washed off before each repainting.

According to one professional fence builder, exterior black latex paint works well. Another option is an asphalt-based paint that costs considerably less than latex, but requires more gallons to get the job done. Find out what's available in your area, and figure your cost on the estimated coverage of a 5-gallon bucket. You might also investigate the cost of a professional spray job by a painting contractor. However, hand painting with brushes and rollers lays on thicker coats of paint than a sprayer, and will add durability and longevity to your wood fence.

HIRING A BUILDER

Your plan will help you pick out the right builder.

GONE ARE the days when a group of neighbors, generally under the watchful eye of a master carpenter, would get together for a barn raising. Today, most barns are built by professional contractors. If you plan to build your own barn, I applaud you and encourage you. Building is an extremely satisfying experience, and a modest horse barn is a project that can be accomplished with fairly basic carpentry skills. However, if you're like most people, you probably lack either the time, tools, or experience required to build your horse facilities alone. In this case, you'll be looking to hire a professional. Following are some recommendations on how to find a good builder, how to avoid some pitfalls in the building process, and how to make the building experience more beneficial for both you and the contractor you hire.

Types of Builders

There are essentially three types of barn builders: individuals or small local companies that specialize in custom barns or small buildings; general contractors who build homes or commercial structures; and national building companies that focus on agricultural buildings generally, perhaps with an emphasis on or specialization in horse facilities.

Locals

Local barn companies are often headed by individuals who are either horsemen who learned the construction trades, or carpenters who developed an interest in horses. They may have an office, or they may operate out of their homes.

An advantage of choosing a small barn building company is that you usually end up dealing directly with the builder. Although the local barn builder will have his own personal building style, there's lots of room to customize designs to get exactly what you want. Because his overhead and advertising costs are usually low, he may be able to build at a much lower cost than either a national firm or a general contractor.

On the negative side, small independent builders usually can't offer financing, which means working with a lender or dipping into savings. Because of limited staff or other constraints, the small local company may be incapable of tackling large facilities. During the busy season, a small company with a reputation for quality may have more business than it can handle. This can mean a delay of weeks or months before there is time in the schedule to complete your building. Furthermore, a small independent builder may be unwilling to work as a general contractor, which can mean that you'll have to also take on the responsibilities of hiring subcontractors to carry out site preparation, electrical wiring, plumbing, and perhaps painting. You also have to coordinate the efforts and schedules of these subcontractors, which can be a real headache.

National or Regional Builders

Prefabricated barns are nothing new. Around the turn of the century, it was possible to order an entire barn—hinges, windows, cupolas, and all—directly from the Sears & Roebuck catalog. Once you'd placed your order and specified necessary modifications or options, the entire barn came shipped in pieces, ready for assembly.

Today, there are numerous national and regional building manufacturers that specialize in agricultural buildings. Steel buildings, in particular, tend to be manufactured by these large firms.

In many cases, these companies offer a variety of designs that can be more or less customized to suit each individual's needs. After meeting with a manufacturer's sales representative and contracting for a particular building, the company will either send their own construction crew to erect the building or they may contract with a local builder to complete the job. The required materials are shipped directly from the manufacturer.

The main advantages of working with a barn or agricultural building manufacturer are that the buildings are generally high in quality and uniform in appearance. Sound engineering and performance-tested materials ensure a solid and long-lasting structure. The buildings are designed with animal and worker safety in mind, and can be among the safest housing for horses.

Some large manufacturers offer financing. Some building designs are a modular arrangement that can be taken apart and moved to a new site, which may offer tax advantages. Some states classify these buildings as farm equipment, which can be depreciated at a faster rate than permanent buildings and may not be subject to property taxes.

On the negative side, most prefab or pre-engineered building manufacturers charge more for their buildings than do independent local builders. Added overhead, such as national advertising, sales commissions, manufacturing costs, and management salaries, add to the final cost that you'll pay. Although the manufacturers save money by producing many of the materials themselves, their finished building might cost up to twice as much as a comparable structure built by an independent local builder.

General Contractors

Sometimes, a general contractor or developer will agree to build a barn along with building a residence. Often, large commercial horse facilities are built by commercial building contractors. Very rarely do commercial or residential contractors take on small, private horse barns, simply because their other work keeps them from becoming involved in these less lucrative projects. Most home builders specialize in stud-frame homes, and may not be familiar with the unique building features and safety requirements of a horse barn. They may prefer to build a stud-frame barn similar to a large garage instead of using the post-and-purlin building style commonly used for pole barn construction.

If you plan to work with a home builder or general contractor, it's best to work from established plans and blueprints to assure that the building you get will be suitable and safe for horses.

Getting Estimates

Just as with any major purchase, it's worthwhile to really shop for the right barn builder. Once you've determined the basic size of your stable and made a list of the essential details, you should contact the various barn building companies in your area for estimates.

Building estimates are based on a combination of materials, labor costs, overhead, and profit. Commonly, small builders will use a simple formula for their estimates, such as figuring material costs, then doubling that amount to cover labor, profit, and expenses. Another, more involved formula is based on a set price per square foot, depending on the quality of materials specified and the amount of labor anticipated. In the case of large commercial facilities, a construction estimator may be called in to determine the project cost.

Some large manufacturers offer financing.

Unless you are working from a building plan or blueprint, it is important to obtain a materials list that specifies how and where the materials will be used. This helps in comparing estimates from a number of contractors. If two contractors come to you with the same price, yet one plans to use more or better quality materials, it's not hard to see where the better value lies.

As you talk to contractors, make it a point to get references from past clients. If possible, inspect the work of the various contractors and talk to the people who own the barns. What do they like and dislike about their buildings? Have there been any problems? How was their relationship with the builder before, during, and after the building process?

You can size up the builder's construction skills yourself by paying attention to certain details. A friend of mine, himself a master carpenter, once said, "You don't have to know how to build to know if it's built right. But you do have to know how to read a level." If you have a level, take it along. If it's a pole barn, check to make sure the posts are plumb (at 90 degrees to the ground). If poles are used, check the outside walls to make sure they're at 90 degrees. If the poles and posts aren't right, neither is the rest of the building.

Look down the long walls. Are they straight, or can you detect wavering lines? Push on the walls. Do they flex or are they

If the poles and posts aren't right, neither is the rest of the building.

solid? Ideally, exterior walls should be fairly rigid.

Look carefully at the trim. Is it consistent on each side of the building? Is it attractive? Sometimes trim is used to hide mistakes or poor workmanship. Look for unusual or excessive trim work, and ask yourself if it was necessary, or simply added to hide something.

Once you've received some bids and inspected some buildings, you'll be in a good position to decide who to hire. You should have three to five bids, perhaps more. In the bidding process, it's standard to eliminate the highest and lowest bids. The logic is that the highest bidder is overpriced, and the lowest bidder is probably underskilled or using cut-rate materials. As a rule of thumb, this may be true; it may also be true that the highest bidder takes great pride and painstaking care in his work, and the lowest bidder may be more efficient and thrifty than his competitors. This is where personal inspections and recommendations come in handy in deciding who to hire.

Contract Negotiations

Once you've settled on a builder, take care in approaching contract negotiations. No matter how comfortable you feel with the person or company you are about to hire, you need to look out for your interests. In any project, misunderstandings can arise and things can go wrong. If you have already agreed in writing with your contractor on how problems will be handled and conflicts resolved, you'll save a lot of headaches down the road.

Some issues that should be addressed in the contract documents include:

1/ A work schedule and completion date for the project, including what steps will be taken if the work is not completed on time.

2/ The agreed price, a payment schedule, and interest charges for past-due payments. Also, a procedure for handling price changes.

3/ A materials list covering all necessary materials for the project, and a clause that spells out what substitutions will be acceptable.

4/ A basic diagram of the building, illustrating the building layout, material layout, door and window position and construction, and structural details such as beam bracing, wall headers, roof or truss-frame attachment, etc.

5/ An agreement on how subcontractors, such as electricians, plumbers, excavators, painters, will be handled, and paid. Will the builder contract these services, or will the barn owner? What will happen if a subcontractor's work interferes with construction or scheduling? How will damages by subcontractors be handled? Generally, it's worthwhile to contract with subcontractors recommended by the builder. If the contractor chooses his own crew, he'll be more likely to resolve problems with them himself.

But it should be spelled out in your agreement with the contractor as to how the "subs" will be paid. Many a new home or barn owner has been hit with liens filed by unpaid subs, even though the general contractor was paid, and was supposed to have paid the subs. Also, be very careful about paying a contractor any money up front.

In fact, it would be well worth the expense to have your attorney review your contract or agreement with the contractor, before you sign it. This could prevent big problems later on.

6/ A procedure that discusses how plan changes will be addressed.

7/ Insurance requirements, safety responsibilities, and liability.

8/ Procedure and acceptable reasons for terminating the contract.

In some localities, building permits and building inspections may be required. It is the responsibility of the builder to make sure these are handled. The builder must adhere to all related construction codes, covenants, building inspection requirements, and sanitation requirements that apply to equine buildings and facilities in your area.

Also, be very careful about paying a contractor any money up front.

ADDING ON

One horse is apt to lead to another, and another. . . .

CONSTRUCTING an addition to a barn or stable can sometimes be more difficult and expensive than building the original structure, especially if little thought was given to the possibility of an addition at the time the original construction took place. But, most anything is possible with the right know-how and, possibly, a bank loan.

These sequence photos show an addition to an existing center-aisle barn with a gable roof. The barn had three 12 by 12-foot box stalls on the south (left-hand) side of the barn pictured. A tack room and an open area for hay storage occu-

pied the north side.

The owner wished to expand the barn in two directions—to the north, adding a shed for hay storage, and to the east end (the facing end in photo 1). Two facing box stalls would be added on the east end; an additional stall and wash area would be added to the north side, on the other side of the tack room.

One problem: In order to accommodate two 12 by 12-foot stalls on the north side, the north wall would have to be moved outward 2 feet. Photo 1 shows the north-side paneling removed, and 6 by 6-inch support posts in place. The builder

Siding on the north wall has been removed, and support posts have been installed. These posts will support one side of the shed roof.

suggested that the roof-line be slightly broken at that point, to afford more overhead room in the attached shed than the existing angle of the roof would otherwise afford. In addition, the builder excavated the shed floor another 1½ to 2 feet, thus providing even more inside space.

And finally, because the barn is on a slight hillside and was prone to flooding in heavy rains, he cut a drainage ditch to divert water. The entire construction, including roofing with asphalt shingles to match the existing roof, took less than 10 days. Metal Port-A-Stall fronts that matched those on the original three stalls were added, and a three-stall barn became a six-stall barn.

The original siding, plus the sliding door, was carefully removed in the beginning, and then reattached to the new framing.

This shows the retaining wall, made of 6 by 6-inch posts, between the barn's dirt floor and the excavated dirt floor of the new shed. Note that the original 6 by 6 posts, which support the existing barn's roof, will not be removed.

Construction is well under way. Tar paper and shingles are waiting on the existing roof, ready for installation as soon as the addition's roof is up.

*Another view of
the shed area under
construction.*

*The 2 by 6-inch rafters are in place for the shed roof. Metal brackets, attaching each
rafter to the horizontal support, still need to be added.*

Framing on the east end of the barn.

The shed is nearly complete at this point. Siding is being attached.

The nearly completed addition. The broken roofline is obvious at this point; metal flashing will be installed over the seam between original roof and new, prior to the installation of tar paper and shingles.

ASSORTED PLANS

Some sample layouts for barns and acreages.

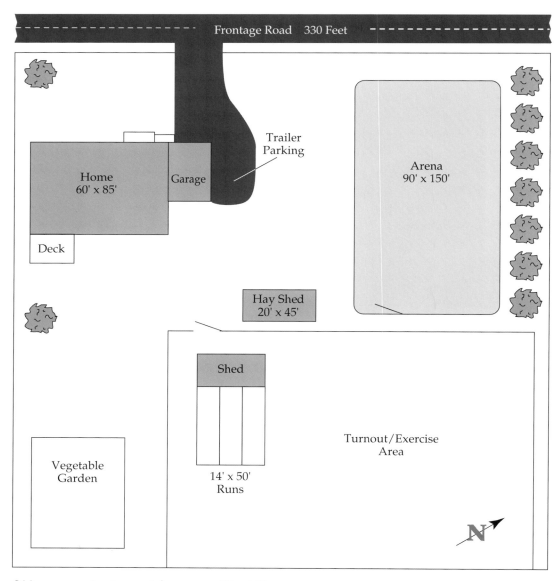

2½-acre private residence.   1" = 59'

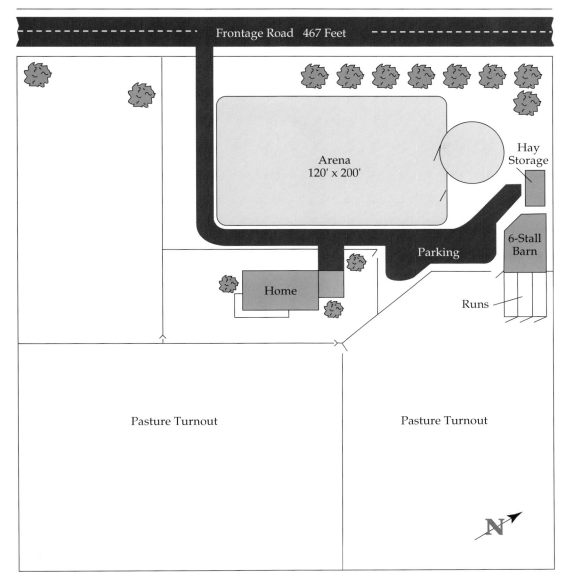

Facilities layout for a 5-acre residence.   1" = 84'

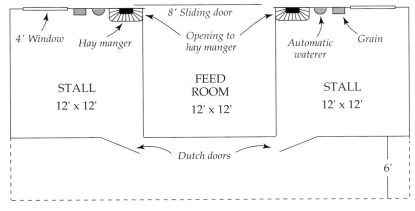

Two stalls and feed room.

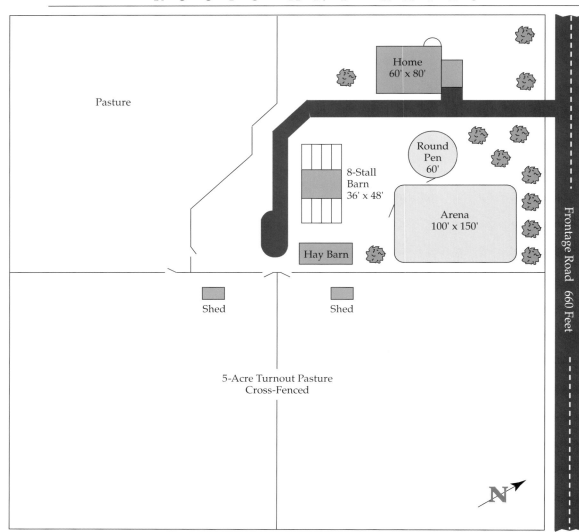

10-acre
private
residence.
1" = 118'

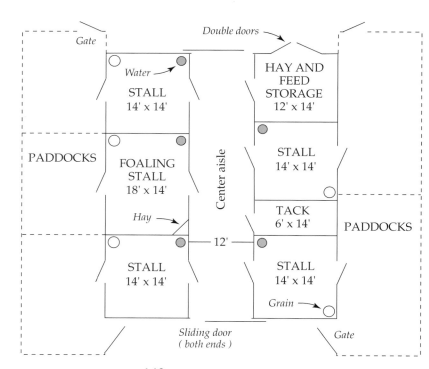

Five stalls,
feed room,
tack room.

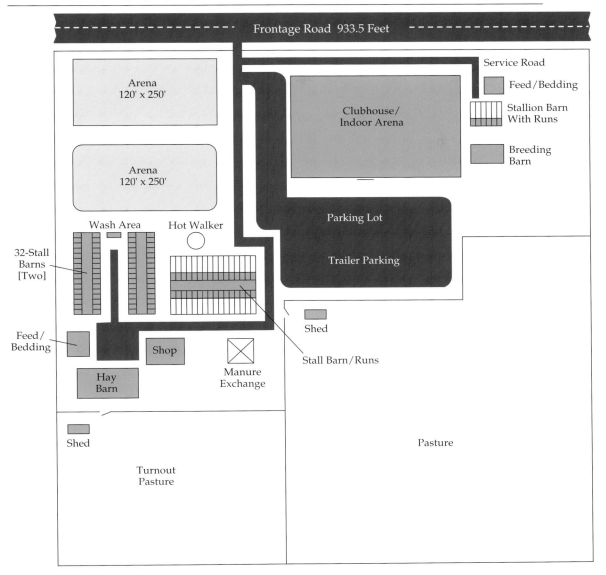

20-acre commercial horse-boarding facility.   1"= 167'

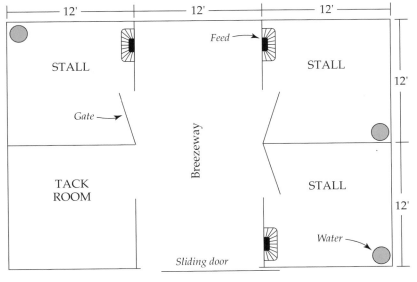

Three stalls
with tack room.

Garages, stalls, and pens.

Four stalls, tack room, and feed storage.

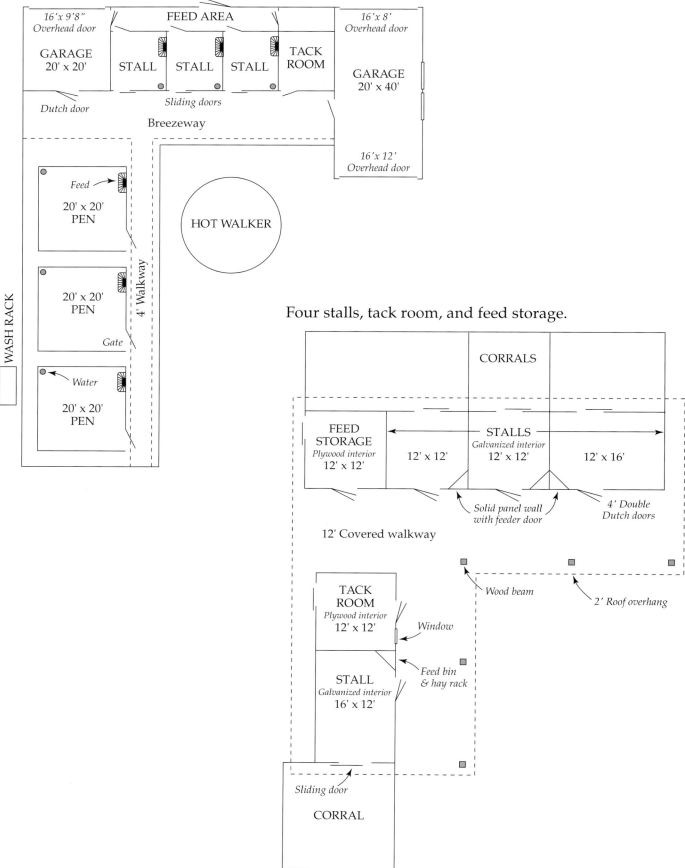

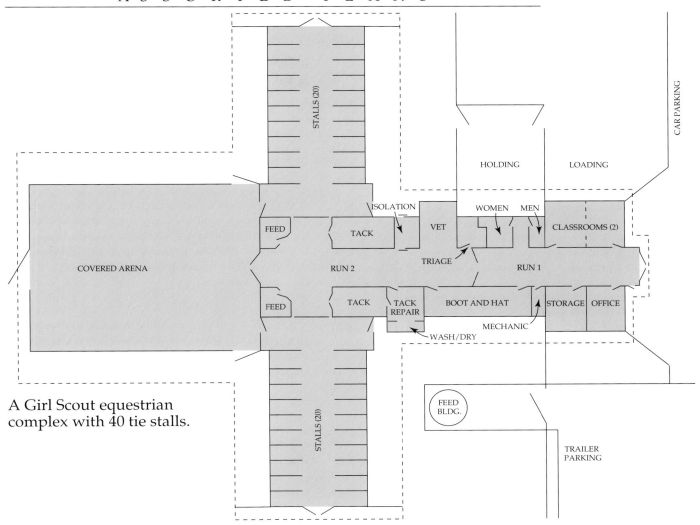

A Girl Scout equestrian complex with 40 tie stalls.

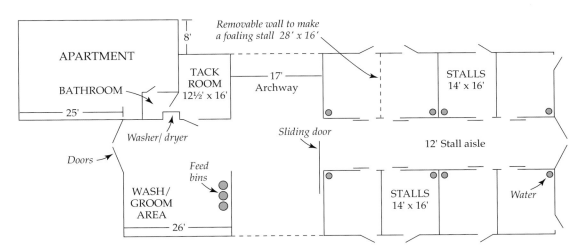

Eight stalls, attached apartment.

The *Western Horseman*, established in 1936, is the world's leading horse publication.
For subscription information: 800-877-5278. To order other *Western Horseman* books: 800-874-6774.
Western Horseman, Box 7980, Colorado Springs, CO 80933-7980.

Books Published by Western Horseman Inc.

BACON & BEANS by Stella Hughes
144 pages and 200-plus recipes for popular western chow.

BARREL RACING by Sharon Camarillo
144 pages and 200 photographs. Tells how to train and compete successfully.

CALF ROPING by Roy Cooper
144 pages and 280 photographs covering the how-to of roping and tying.

CUTTING by Leon Harrel
144 pages and 200 photographs. Complete how-to guide on this popular sport.

FIRST HORSE by Fran Devereux Smith
176 pages, 160 black-and-white photos, about 40 illustrations. Step-by-step, how-to information for the first-time horse owner and/or novice rider.

HEALTH PROBLEMS by Robert M. Miller, D.V.M.
144 pages on management, illness and injuries, lameness, mares and foals, and more.

HORSEMAN'S SCRAPBOOK by Randy Steffen
144 pages and 250 illustrations. A collection of popular handy hints.

IMPRINT TRAINING by Robert M. Miller, D.V.M.
144 pages and 250 photographs. Learn how to "program" newborn foals.

LEGENDS by Diane C. Simmons
168 pages and 214 photographs. Includes these outstanding early-day Quarter Horse stallions and mares: Barbra B, Bert, Chicaro Bill, Cowboy P-12, Depth Charge (TB), Doc Bar, Go Man Go, Hard Twist, Hollywood Gold, Joe Hancock, Joe Reed P-3, Joe Reed II, King P-234, King Fritz, Leo, Peppy, Plaudit, Poco Bueno, Poco Tivio, Queenie, Quick M Silver, Shue Fly, Star Duster, Three Bars (TB), Top Deck (TB), and Wimpy P-1.

LEGENDS 2 by Jim Goodhue, Frank Holmes, Phil Livingston, Diane C. Simmons
192 pages and 224 photographs. Includes these outstanding Quarter Horses: Clabber, Driftwood, Easy Jet, Grey Badger II, Jessie James, Jet Deck, Joe Bailey P-4 (Gonzales), Joe Bailey (Weatherford), King's Pistol, Lena's Bar, Lightning Bar, Lucky Blanton, Midnight, Midnight Jr, Moon Deck, My Texas Dandy, Oklahoma Star, Oklahoma Star Jr., Peter McCue, Rocket Bar (TB), Skipper W, Sugar Bars, and Traveler.

LEGENDS 3 by Jim Goodhue, Frank Holmes, Diane Ciarloni, Kim Guenther, Larry Thornton, Betsy Lynch
208 pages and 196 photographs. Includes these outstanding Quarter Horses: Flying Bob, Hollywood Jac 86, Jackstraw (TB), Maddon's Bright Eyes, Mr Gun Smoke, Old Sorrel, Piggin String (TB), Poco Lena, Poco Pine, Poco Dell, Question Mark, Quo Vadis, Royal King, Showdown, Steel Dust, and Two Eyed Jack.

NATURAL HORSE-MAN-SHIP by Pat Parelli
224 pages and 275 photographs. Parelli's six keys to a natural horse-human relationship.

REINING, Completely Revised by Al Dunning
216 pages and over 300 photographs showing how to train horses for this popular event.

ROOFS AND RAILS by Gavin Ehringer
144 pages, 128 black-and-white photographs plus drawings, charts, and floor plans. How to plan and build your ideal horse facility.

STARTING COLTS by Mike Kevil
168 pages and 400 photographs. Step-by-step process in starting colts.

THE HANK WIESCAMP STORY by Frank Holmes
208 pages and over 260 photographs. The biography of the legendary breeder of Quarter Horses, Appaloosas, and Paints.

TEAM PENNING by Phil Livingston
144 pages and 200 photographs. Tells how to compete in this popular family sport.

TEAM ROPING by Leo Camarillo
144 pages and 200 photographs covering every aspect of heading and heeling.

WELL-SHOD by Don Baskins
160 pages, 300 black-and-white photos and illustrations. A horseshoeing guide for owners and farriers. The easy-to-read text, illustrations, and photos show step-by-step how to trim and shoe a horse for a variety of uses. Special attention is paid to corrective shoeing techniques for horses with various foot and leg problems.

WESTERN HORSEMANSHIP by Richard Shrake
144 pages and 150 photographs. Complete guide to riding western horses.

WESTERN TRAINING by Jack Brainard
With Peter Phinny. 136 pages. Stresses the foundation for western training.